Wittgenstein,
Grammar and God

ALAN KEIGHTLEY

Wittgenstein, Grammar and God

London
EPWORTH PRESS

Enquiries should be addressed to
The Methodist Publishing House
Wellington Road
Wimbledon
London SW19 8EU

7162 0264 6

Printed in Great Britain by
Ebenezer Baylis and Son Limited
The Trinity Press, Worcester, and London

FOR JOAN

5-21-85

Acknowledgements

The author and publisher are grateful for permission to quote from the following:

Tractatus Logico-Philosophicus, Ludwig Wittgenstein; *Without Answers* and *Discussions of Wittgenstein*, Rush Rhees; *The Concept of Prayer* and *Faith and Philosophical Enquiry*, D. Z. Phillips; *Morality and Purpose*, J. L. Stocks; *Gravity and Grace*, Simone Weil; *Ethics and Action*, Peter Winch; *Cause and Meaning in the Social Sciences*, Ernest Gellner; all Routledge & Kegan Paul Ltd.

Models for Divine Activity, Ian T. Ramsey; *Words About God*, ed. Ian T. Ramsey; *Thinking About God*, John Macquarrie; *The Reality of God*, S. Ogden; *Theological Explorations*, Paul van Buren; all S.C.M. Press Ltd.

Christian Empiricism, Ian T. Ramsey, Sheldon Press.

Notebooks 1914–1916, *Lectures and Conversations on Aesthetics, Psychology and Religious Belief*, *Letters to Russell, Keynes and Moore*, *Remarks on the Foundations of Mathematics*, *Philosophical Grammar*, *Philosophical Investigations*, *Zettel*, *Blue and Brown Books*, *On Certainty*, Ludwig Wittgenstein; *Letters from Ludwig Wittgenstein with a Memoir*, Paul Engelmann; *Wittgenstein's Conception of Philosophy*, K. T. Fann; *Induction and Deduction*, I. Dilman; *Religion and Understanding*, ed. D. Z. Phillips; all Basil Blackwell Ltd.

Wittgenstein's Vienna, A. Janik and S. Toulmin, Weidenfeld & Nicolson.

The Prose For God, eds. I. Gregor and W. Stein, Sheed & Ward.

A Rumour of Angels, Peter L. Berger; *The Way of Transcendence*, A. Kee; *Gorgias*, Plato; all reprinted by permission of Penguin Books Ltd.

Reason and Commitment, Roger Trigg; *The Survival of English*,

Ian Robinson; *Philosophy* journal; all Cambridge University Press.

Ludwig Wittgenstein: A Memoir, Norman Malcolm; *New Essays on Religious Language*, ed. D. M. High; Oxford University Press.

The Heythrop Journal, *The Human World*, *Encounter*, *Mind*, *The Tablet*, *The Philosophical Review*, the trustees of Ludwig Wittgenstein's estate.

Philosophical Books. *The Tragic Sense of Life*, Miguel de Unamuno; *Death and Immortality*, D. Z. Phillips; *Contemporary Critiques of Religion*, Kai Nielsen; *God and the Universe of Faiths*, *Faith and Knowledge*, John H. Hick; *Faith and the Philosophers*, ed. John H. Hick; *The Private Language Argument*, ed. O. R. Jones; all Macmillan (London & Basingstoke).

Modern British Philosophy, Bryan Magee, Secker & Warburg. John H. Hick, *Philosophy of Religion*, 2nd ed. © 1973, p. 96, reprinted by permission of Prentice-Hall, Inc., Englewood Cliffs, New Jersey, U.S.A.

Selected Essays and Notebooks, Albert Camus Copyright © by Albert Camus, Hamish Hamilton, London. *The Myth of Sisyphus and Other Essays*, Albert Camus, translated by Justin O'Brien, Alfred A. Knopf, Inc., New York, and Copyright © 1955 by Albert Camus, Hamish Hamilton, London.

The Autobiography of Bertrand Russell; *Philosophical Papers*, G. E. Moore; *Prospect for Metaphysics*, ed. Ian T. Ramsey; all George Allen & Unwin Ltd. *The Structure of Scientific Revolutions*, 2nd ed. enlarged, 1970, T. S. Kuhn, University of Chicago Press.

Contents

CONTENTS

Preface

THIS IS not a book for the connoisseurs of Wittgenstein. It is an attempt to introduce students, theologians and the interested general reader to the significance of Wittgenstein's philosophy for religious belief. Nevertheless, any study of this kind must enter into dialogue with people who have already given several years thought to the matter. This field is a hotly disputed and confusing one in contemporary philosophy of religion, and this book may help to clear up some of the ground for people unfamiliar with this way of thinking.

I believe that the issues are vital and concern theologians just as much as philosophers. Chapter six might provide a reason for working through the first five chapters for those interested in theology's stake in the matter. For the more philosophically minded, chapters one and two discuss Wittgenstein's philosophy in relation to religious belief. Chapter three concentrates in detail on D. Z. Phillips' application of Wittgenstein's ideas to religion, and chapter four attempts to clarify some of the questions which have accumulated up to that point. Chapter five, on reductionism, directs the discussion towards the more theological issues dealt with in chapter six. Any religion could be studied from a Wittgensteinian standpoint, but I usually have Christianity in mind when I refer to 'religion' or 'religious belief'.

My interest in these questions originated in doctoral studies at Birmingham University under the supervision of Professor John Hick. I have also learned a great deal from conversations with Professor D. Z. Phillips. My friends, Graham Fergusson, Martin Evan-Jones, John Norris and Neil McDonald have patiently discussed and stimulated my thoughts on these matters. I am particularly grateful to Martin Evans-Jones for providing many English translations from the Welsh. My wife, Joan, has heard it all before but has never complained.

Abbreviations

I HAVE used the following abbreviations in the text. Full details can be found in the bibliography.

Wittgenstein, Ludwig

	T.	*Tractatus Logico—Philosophicus*
	P.I.	*Philosophical Investigations* (references to Part 1 are by paragraph numbers, e.g., *P.I.* 23, and to Part 2 by page numbers, e.g., *P.I.* p. 210)
	B.B.B.	*The Blue and Brown Books*
	R.F.M.	*Remarks on the Foundations of Mathematics*
	L.C.	*Lectures and Conversations on Aesthetics, Psychology and Religious Belief*
	O.C.	*On Certainty*
	Z.	*Zettel*
	N.B. *1914–16*	*Notebooks 1914–1916*
	R.F.G.B.	*'Remarks on Frazer's "Golden Bough"'*
	P.G.	*Philosophical Grammar*
Phillips, Dewi Z.	C.P.	*The Concept of Prayer*
	F.P.E.	*Faith and Philosophical Enquiry*
	D.I.	*Death and Immortality*
	R.U.	*Religion and Understanding*
	M.P.	*Moral Practices*

Wittgenstein's Advice to a Distraught Fly

IN SOME theological circles, Wittgenstein is thought of as philosophy's 'bogey man', threatening the faithful in much the same way as theology's Rudolf Bultmann. Neither man deserves this reputation. This book, however, is mainly about the influence of Wittgenstein, and it will achieve something if it dissuades anyone from associating Wittgenstein with the sceptical approach of A. J. Ayer, Antony Flew, etc. On the other hand, in some philosophical circles it is part of the folklore that Wittgenstein's work 'tolerates' any and every kind of religious belief. This view may stem from the impression created by some of Wittgenstein's own more cryptic remarks. G. E. M. Anscombe reports that Wittgenstein said the following about his own later work:

> Its advantage is that if you believe, say, Spinoza or Kant, this interferes with what you can believe in religion; but if you believe me, nothing of the sort.[1]

It depends, of course, what kind of religion he had in mind. Anscombe wisely added[2] that she did not know whether Wittgenstein was right about the influence of his own philosophy. Whatever may be the truth about this, Wittgenstein's general influence upon the *study* of religious belief cannot seriously be doubted. This influence has permeated all modern studies in the philosophy of religion. Wittgenstein, together with philosophers like G. E. Moore, J. L. Austin and John Wisdom, has been instrumental in discrediting Logical Positivism, the 'old Adam' of Analysis,

---

[1] 'Misinformation: What Wittgenstein Really Said,' *The Tablet*, April 17th, 1954, p. 373.
[2] Ibid., p. 373.

and in putting forward an altogether richer concept of meaning. The following comment from Wittgenstein's lectures in 1930–33 is a terse summary of this rejection of positivism: 'The meaning of a word is no longer for us an object corresponding to it.'[3] The force of this rejection has been felt in many ways by philosophers. It has created a general style of philosophizing whereby philosophers see the necessity of placing words and concepts within their immediate verbal and social contexts and of giving a description of what they see.

In considering Wittgenstein's work I shall attempt to keep one eye on theology's problems as well as those in the philosophy of religion. Some theologians[4] have tried to apply Wittgenstein's ideas directly to theology. I shall concentrate in some detail, however, on a group of philosophers whom we could well call the 'devout Wittgensteinians'.[5] Rush Rhees, Norman Malcolm, D. Z. Phillips and Peter Winch form the core of this group. These philosophers stand out as a special group either because they were, like Rhees and Malcolm, Wittgenstein's own students, or because, like Phillips and Winch, they have been closely associated with the independent work of Wittgenstein's pupils.

The most exhaustive work on religious belief has, in fact, come from 'third generation' Wittgensteinians, and primarily from the pen of D. Z. Phillips. Phillips has taken Wittgenstein's ideas very radically to heart, and I have thought it worthwhile to consider his contribution in detail. His work, it seems to me, represents a genuine and promising option in contemporary philosophy of religion. There is certainly something very appealing about Wittgenstein's philosophy. It may be that Wittgenstein's method

---

[3] G. E. Moore, 'Wittgenstein's Lectures in 1930–33', *Mind*, Jan. 1954, Vol. 63, p. 9.

[4] Paul van Buren, Paul L. Holmer, Dallas M. High, W. Hordern, etc.— see bibliography.

[5] See A. G. N. Flew, 'Anthropology and Rationality', *Question*, 5, 1972, p. 95.

offers the prospect of bringing what he called 'peace' to philosophy.[6] 'Peace' would presumably come to the analyst of religious belief, on the Wittgensteinian view, if he gave up the attempt to gaze, as it were, into the bright blue metaphysical yonder, and came to grips with the *grammar* of what is readily to hand.

This study is primarily about the *grammar* of belief. I hope the meaning of this phrase will become clear later. There is a sense in which theology itself is the 'grammar of belief', and I shall attempt, as I said earlier, to keep an eye on current problems in theology. Paul Tillich has said that every theologian must in some sense be a philosopher. Wittgenstein's philosophy may, in fact, help to ease the theologians' 'mental cramps' as well as the philosopher's. Whatever the prevailing theologies, whether they be of the secular, of hope, of play, etc., it will always be important to know the character of the *grammar* they assume; what sort of 'reference'—if any—is ascribed to 'God', and so on.

Wittgenstein was a formidable thinker by any standards. Yet he insisted that there was a sense in which philosophy is 'simple':

> Why is philosophy so complicated? It ought to be altogether simple. Philosophy unties those knots in our thinking which we have unwittingly put there; however, this requires movements as complicated as the knots. Though philosophy's result is simple, its method, if it is to arrive at that result, cannot be. The complexity of philosophy is not in its subject matter but rather in our knotted understanding.[7]

Later, in the *Investigations*, Wittgenstein expressed a similar idea when he asked himself, 'What is your aim in philosophy?', and answered, 'To shew the fly the way out of the fly-bottle.'[8] To develop the same metaphor, we could

[6] *P.I.*, 133.
[7] *Philosophische Bemerkungen* (Blackwell, Oxford, 1964), p. 52. I have used Paul L. Holmer's translation—see D. M. High (ed.), *New Essays on Religious Language* (O.U.P., New York, 1969), p. 25.
[8] *P.I.*, 309.

say that, following Wittgenstein, D. Z. Phillips sees most modern philosophers of religion as being in a similar position to the fly who is struggling to force his way through the wrong end of the fly-bottle—a hopeless task. Phillips is trying to convince the fly that there is a way out which has been open all along, if only it will change direction and see. The direction in which Phillips is asking his fellow philosophers to look will constitute one of the main topics for discussion in the chapters which follow.

The literature on Wittgenstein is massive and it is discouraging even to the scholars who attempt to keep up. We must pay attention, however briefly, to some of the issues which are still controversial in Wittgenstein's philosophy, as well as enter into dialogue with writers who have already given considerable thought to its application to religion. It is not possible here to embark on a quest for the 'historical Wittgenstein', particularly concerning his views of religion.[9] Even where Wittgenstein mentions religion directly in his writings we have to tread very warily. In almost all of what Wittgenstein writes, whatever the subject matter, he is writing about logic. Some biographical references, however, will be inevitable. No one who reads accounts of Wittgenstein's life, the sacrifice of his fortune, detestation of pretense, etc., can fail to be moved. One of Wittgenstein's early friends, Paul Engelmann, goes so far as to say that Wittgenstein's life and work shows the possibility of a 'new spiritual attitude'.[10] There is no need to dismiss this claim out of hand as the pious hope of a sentimental friend. There is something very compelling about Wittgenstein's life and work.

The fact that the Wittgensteinians' approach has behind it the work of a very strong minded philosophy, and that their master enjoys the unquestioned respect of most living philosophers, should encourage us to pay them close atten-

[9] See bibliography for writings by A. Janik, S. Toulmin, P. Engelmann, W. W. Bartley III.

[10] P. Engelmann, *Letters from Ludwig Wittgenstein with a Memoir* (Blackwell, Oxford, 1967), p. 135.

tion. It would be unnecessary to say this were it not for the fact that the Wittgensteinian view is sometimes summarily dismissed as another brand of reductionism or confusingly classified as 'Wittgensteinian Fideism'. There is a sense in which the chief thrust of the Wittgensteinian approach is *against* reductionism. It raises the whole question of just what reductionism is in religion.

CHAPTER ONE

Religious Belief
and Wittgenstein's Philosophy

MALCOLM TELLS us[1] that Wittgenstein once concluded a
year's lectures with the following: 'The only seed that I am
likely to sow is a certain jargon.' Those words were uttered
in 1939 and have proved to be an accurate gloss on much of
the philosophy done in the thirty years which followed. The
aphoristic and apparent unsystematic form of his later philosophy may have made his work vulnerable to such treatment. Wittgenstein's frequent complaint that his work was
misunderstood also seems warranted.[2] Even the *Tractatus*,
his most 'systematic' work, was mistakenly taken as a
classical work of Logical Positivism. In that case, however,
Wittgenstein was alive to dissociate himself from the ideas
of the Vienna Circle and make Carnap realize, after several
conversations, that he was not 'one of us'.[3] One can only
speculate about the kind of reaction which would have been
evoked from Wittgenstein by the controversy surrounding
his name in the philosophy of religion today. I therefore
proceed from this point in great fear and trembling.

The 'jargon' which has become compulsory for a discussion of the present kind, namely, 'forms of life', 'language-
games', 'grammar', etc., is only intelligible within the total
context of Wittgenstein's life's work. A brief outline of this
is provided first of all. The remaining sections of this and the
next chapter discuss some of the basic themes in Wittgenstein's work, particularly as they relate to the study of religion. Some of the difficulties which arise directly from

1   N. Malcolm, *Ludwig Wittgenstein*; A Memoir (O.U.P., London, 1967), p. 63.
2   Ibid., p. 59.
3   See Carnap's 'Autobiography' in P. Schlipp (ed.), *The Philosophy of
Carnap* (Open Court, La Salle, Illinois), 1964.

Wittgenstein's views will be treated in the discussion of D. Z. Phillips to avoid over-burdening the exposition of Wittgenstein's own work.

There is a certain artificiality in any *general* account of Wittgenstein's philosophy. The real value of this way of philosophizing is only evident when we see how it applies to particular problems. It is essential for the present purposes, however, to have some idea of Wittgenstein's treatment of language in general, if only to provide a supportive background to what we may eventually judge to be his view of religious language in particular.

Wittgenstein's Early and Later Philosophy

For modern analytical philosophers, the question of the *meaning* of religious belief comes before the problem of its *truth* or *falsity*. One concept of meaning which has been very influential in that tradition of philosophy is that found in Wittgenstein's *Philosophical Investigations*. In this he offers an idea of meaning in terms of language-games and forms of life, and at the same time corrects his earlier concept of meaning in the *Tractatus*.

His earlier view is usually called the 'Picture theory' of meaning.[4] A proposition, says Wittgenstein, 'pictures' a situation in the world.[5] The terms 'objects' and 'names' denoted the elements which comprise reality and a proposition, respectively. 'Objects make up the substance of the world',[6] 'objects' being a technical term for the ultimate constituents of the world. These 'objects' are 'simples' and cannot be further analysed; they can be referred to only by being named. Similarly, 'names' are logically proper names which simply designate, but do not describe, their referents. This view of language is at the heart of his earlier

---

[4] There are many exhaustive expositions of this. It is only possible to provide a very brief summary here.

[5] *T.*, 4.01; *N.B. 1914–16*, p. 25.

[6] *T.*, 2.021.

theory, i.e., the meaning of language is that to which it *refers*.

Wittgenstein's theory was not based on empirical investigation but on logical analysis. He was indifferent to actual examples of 'names' or 'objects'. For language to have a determinate, precise meaning, these simples (objects and names) must, logically, exist. A configuration of 'names' in a proposition mirrored the configuration of 'objects' in the world. This is what Wittgenstein meant by 'logical form', i.e., 'What any picture, of whatever form, must have in common with reality, in order to be able to depict it—correctly or incorrectly—in any way at all, is logical form, i.e., the form or reality.'[7] To determine whether or not a proposition is true or false, one has to 'compare it with reality'.[8]

This theory of meaning is rejected in the *Investigations*. Wittgenstein rejects the notion that both the proposition and its referent must have an identical logical form. He made several criticisms of his Picture theory, but one of the major criticisms was a rejection of the idea that the 'simples' in the proposition and the world must correspond absolutely. His earlier view had been inadequate.[9] Wittgenstein also challenges his earlier notion that a proposition must have an absolutely determinate sense.[10] But the belief—basic to his earlier view—that the meaning of language is that to which it refers, is also radically changed. It was a consequence of the earlier view that a word is meaningless if nothing corresponds to it in reality. But Wittgenstein argues in the following way in the *Investigations*: 'When Mr N. N. dies one says that the bearer of the name dies, not that the meaning dies.'[11]

The *Tractatus*, in fact, had imposed upon language a particular idea of meaning. Wittgenstein came to very

[7] T., 2.18.
[8] T., 2.223.
[9] P.I., 47.
[10] P.I., 88.
[11] P.I., 40.

different conclusions when, as he claimed, he overcame 'prejudice' and looked to see to what *uses* language is put. His later method of doing philosophy began to emerge during the lectures at Cambridge, 1930–33.[12] Wittgenstein says in the Preface to the *Investigations*, dated 1945, that the book contains work which had occupied him 'for the last sixteen years', i.e., since 1929.[13]

The Blue and Brown Books (1933–35) clearly show a fundamental change in Wittgenstein's philosophy. From Waismann's notes we learn that Wittgenstein had become disillusioned with logical symbolism as a means of describing the scope and significance of actual linguistic behaviour.[14] On July 1st, 1932, Wittgenstein said to Waismann: 'In the *Tractatus* I was unclear about "logical analysis" and the clarification it suggests. At that time I thought that it provided a "connexion between Language and Reality".'[15]

In the *Tractatus* Wittgenstein had been concerned solely with a formal analysis of the *picturing* or *representational* function of language. He had neglected the way language is *actually* put to *use* in human life. As a consequence of his dissatisfaction, in his later work he faced the problem of how *any* piece of language—pictorial or otherwise—gains significance by its use. Hence, as Rush Rhees notes,[16] Wittgenstein is now occupied by entirely new categories, namely, 'language-games', 'learning a language', 'systems of communication', 'the study of primitive forms of language', etc. The use of the new categories marked the beginning of what is sometimes called Wittgenstein's 'linguistic turn'. The turn is fully completed in the *Investigations*: ' "sentence" and

---

[12] Some record of these survives in a series of articles which G. E. Moore wrote for *Mind*, Vol. 63, 1954, pp. 1–15; 289–316; Vol. 64 1955, pp. 1–27.

[13] *P.I.*, p. vii.

[14] F. Waismann, *Ludwig Wittgenstein und der Wiener Kreis*, (Blackwell, Oxford, 1967); see under Waismann's heading 'Uber Dogmatismus', 9th Dec. 1931, p. 182f.

[15] Ibid., pp. 209f. (S. Toulmin's translation—'Ludwig Wittgenstein' *Encounter*, Jan. 1969, p. 62).

[16] B.B.B., p. ix.

"language" has not the formal unity that I imagined, but is the family of structures more or less related to one another . . . The *preconceived idea* of crystalline purity can only be removed by turning our whole examination round.'[17]

Thus language does not acquire meaning through some hidden essence or from any *essentially* 'pictorial' character. It acquires meaning from the various procedures through which we give it particular uses in the course of our common life. Consequently, for the later Wittgenstein language is seen as a formative element in the social life of man which must be *described* in all its great variety: 'Philosophy may in no way interfere with the actual use of language; it can in the end only describe it. For it cannot give it any foundation either. It leaves everything as it is';[18] and, 'We must do away with all *explanation*, and description alone must take its place.'[19] Philosophy can in no way *prescribe* what is rationally possible on the basis of an independent framework of reality. No one can draw up a limit *a priori* to the number or kinds of possibilities in language. Philosophy must simply describe these possibilities.

At one point, Wittgenstein provides a neat summary of his own programme of work: 'What we are supplying are really remarks on the natural history of man: not curiosities however, but rather observations on facts which no one has doubted and which have only gone unremarked because they are always before our eyes.'[20] Indeed, when one takes a 'wider look round'[21] without the preconceived idea of looking for '*one* comprehensive essence',[22] one is surprised by the great diversity in language use. Thus Wittgenstein speaks of 'games' to combat this craving for an overall unity. There are connections between the different uses, countless 'family

---

[17] *P.I.*, 108.
[18] *P.I.*, 124.
[19] *P.I.*, 109; see *B.B.B.*, p. 18.
[20] *R.F.M.* I-141, p. 43; cf. *P.I.*, 129.
[21] *R.F.M.* II-1, p. 54.
[22] *Z.*, 444.

resemblances', but not necessarily something common to all.

In the following two sections I shall attempt to fill out this bare outline by relating important aspects of the early and later work to the assessment of religious belief.

Religion in the early period—'the Mystical' and the Transcendental Values

In the final sections of the *Tractatus* Wittgenstein discusses the 'transcendental', 'the ineffable' and 'the mystical' in close connection with comments about ethics, aesthetics and religion. The *Tractatus* itself concludes with the famous sentence: 'What we cannot speak about we must pass over in silence.'[23] Here are a few of the direct references to the mystical which culminate in this conclusion:

6.44   It is not *how* things are in the world that is mystical, but *that* it exists.

6.45   To view the world sub specie aeterni is to view it as a whole—a limited whole.
    Feeling the world as a limited whole—it is this that is mystical.

6.522   There are, indeed, things that cannot be put into words. They *make themselves manifest*. They are what is mystical.

and 6.432 is very closely related to these passages:

How things are in the world is a matter of complete indifference for what is higher. God does not reveal himself *in* the world.

The precise meaning of these passages is still controversial. Less controversial now is their relation to Logical Positivism. On a positivist reading the final sentence of the *Tractatus* could be taken as an injunction to keep silence *because* what would otherwise be uttered is unimportant as well as nonsensical. The final passages on this view are dismissed as *obiter dicta*. We have cogent reasons now, how-

[23]   *T.*, 7.

ever, for thinking that Wittgenstein himself held the opposite view. For example, at the time the *Tractatus* was written Wittgenstein corresponded with his friend, Ludwig Ficker, and on one occasion wrote to him about its purpose:

> *The book's point is an ethical one.* I once meant to include in the preface a sentence which is not in fact there now, but which I will write out for you here, because it will perhaps be a key to the work for you. What I meant to write, then, was this: My work consists of two parts: the one presented here plus all that I have *not* written. And *it is precisely this second part that is the important one.*[24]

This view of the *Tractatus* is confirmed by Wittgenstein's letters to another friend, Paul Engelmann, and the latter's own memoir.[25] Nevertheless, it is possible to avoid the positivist mistake of treating the final sections as curious addenda and yet to regard the question of the mystical in purely logical terms, namely, by seeing the mystical solely in terms of the ineffable relation between language and the world. Wittgenstein's discussion of the nature of language and the function of propositions explains how we can make literal and meaningful statements, but it does not give us a literal account of this linguistic function itself. This has to be *shown* by a metaphor or a myth. The *Tractatus* as a whole should have served this purpose. Wittgenstein speaks of the

---

[24] L. Wittgenstein, Briefe an Ludwig von Ficker, in Brenner Studien; quoted by A. Janik and S. Toulmin, *Wittgenstein's Vienna* (Weidenfeld & Nicolson, London, 1973), p. 192.

[25] See especially pp. 97ff. Indirect confirmation is given in Waismann's notes ('Notes on Talks with Wittgenstein' *Philosophy Today*, No. 1, ed. J. H. Gill (Macmillan, 1968), pp. 14–19) of conversations with Wittgenstein during 1929 and 1930, and Wittgenstein's own 'Lecture on Ethics' (see *Philosophy Today*, No. 1, pp. 4–14). The whole cultural background to Wittgenstein's 'ethical purpose' has been stressed by A. Janik and S. Toulmin (*Wittgenstein's Vienna*). Carnap, a member of the Vienna Circle, comments: 'When we were reading Wittgenstein's book in the Circle, I had erroneously believed that his attitude towards metaphysics was similar to ours. I had not paid sufficient attention to the statements in his book about the mystical, because his feelings and thoughts in this area were too divergent from mine.' (Quoted by K. T. Fann, *Wittgenstein's Conception of Philosophy* (Blackwell, Oxford, 1969), p. 36.)

Tractatus as a 'ladder' which one must discard once one has climbed it.[26] In the *Tractatus* the relation between language and the world is itself ineffable. The propositions cannot refer to *how* they refer. They would be self-referential and meaningless.

The concluding sentence, 'What we cannot speak about we must pass over in silence', would therefore be apposite to the way logical form—what propositions have in common with reality in order to be able to represent it—is ineffable. But to interpret the *Tractatus* solely in this way would be to see it as an expression of, to borrow a phrase, 'syntactical mysticism'.[27] But it is not *only* logic which is 'transcendental' in the *Tractatus*. Ethics too is transcendental.[28] In fact, there is a whole group of ideas concerned with the extra-logical sense of the transcendental, e.g., 'The sense of the world';[29] 'the world of the happy . . . and . . . the unhappy';[30] 'the riddle of life';[31] 'God', as in 'God does not reveal himself *in* the world';[32] 'ethics' and 'aesthetics'.[33] Irving's 'syntactical mysticism' does less than justice to these kinds of expressions; that is, where Wittgenstein's comments about the mystical are interpreted simply as a natural outcome of a doctrine he held in pure logic.[34] It is, of course, possible to try to do justice to the above expressions in the *Tractatus* without necessarily concluding that the mystical in this extra-logical sense is part of what is meant by *religious* mysticism. In different ways Zemach and McGuinness have argued precisely this.[35]

---

[26] *T.*, 6.54–7.
[27] J. A. Irving, 'Mysticism and the Limits of Communication' in A. P. Stiernotte (ed.), *Mysticism and the Modern Mind* (The Liberal Arts Press, New York, 1959), pp. 99–112.
[28] *T.*, 6.421.
[29] *T.*, 6.41.
[30] *T.*, 6.43.
[31] *T.*, 6.4312.
[32] *T.*, 6.432.
[33] *T.*, 6.421.
[34] Ibid., p. 111.
[35] E. Zemach ('Wittgenstein's Philosophy of the Mystical' in I. M. Copi

Without trying to identify 'the mystical' in the *Tractatus* too closely with religion, let us briefly consider the logical status to which Wittgenstein appears to assign religious belief in his very early period. According to the *Tractatus*, no proposition can be of greater or lesser value than another: 'All propositions are of equal value.'[36] Propositions are simply concerned with the facts and with relations which hold among the ultimately simple objects in the world. The *sense* of the world itself—what value we can ascribe to it—is a different matter. We cannot ascribe value to propositions. Neither can they express value:

6.41   The sense of the world must lie outside the world. In the world everything is as it is, and everything happens as it does happen: *in* it no value exists—and if it did exist, it would have no value.

---

and G. W. Beard ed., *Essays on Wittgenstein's Tractatus* (Routledge and Kegan Paul, London, 1966) pp. 359–75) considers the terms 'God', 'voice of God', 'the purpose of existence', etc., in the *Tractatus* and *Notebooks* to be fanciful phraseology (p. 371). God is simply a word for 'Fate', 'world', or 'the general form of the proposition' (pp. 361 & 365). Zemach sees Wittgenstein's acceptance of the grim inevitability of fate as 'the bitter truth behind this fanciful phraseology': 'The religious mask appears very thin, behind which the Schopenhauerian pessimism is clearly visible' (p. 371). Zemach makes no attempt to put the mystical against the wider background of Wittgenstein's life and work. B. F. McGuinness ('The Mysticism of the *Tractatus*' *Philosophical Review* (1966), Vol. 75, pp. 305–28) does, however, relate the mysticism of the *Tractatus* to its biographical context and the influence of Tolstoy. McGuinness thinks that the *Tractatus* is 'mystical' in the sense that 'there is a common enough mystical state which has little to do with religion' (p. 326). There is sense, he argues, in speaking of a 'single quasi-experiential ground for logic, ethics, mysticism and solipsism', although this experience may be 'merely implicit in the case of logic and at its height in the case of seeing what the meaning of life is' (p. 311). For McGuinness, Wittgenstein's mysticism is neither Christian nor theistic. Where parallels exist to Wittgenstein's mysticism they are to be found in the varieties of nature mysticism described in the writings of R. C. Zaehner and William James. McGuinness tries to find a close relation between Wittgenstein's 'mysticism' and Russell's essay, 'Mysticism and Logic'. However, as Janik and Toulmin have argued, the circumstances surrounding the young Wittgenstein were those of Vienna as it was in the last decades of the Habsburg monarchy and not those of the post-Idealist English philosophical circles.

[36]   *T.*, 6.4.

> If there is any value that does have value, it must lie outside the whole sphere of what happens and is the case. For all that happens and is the case is accidental.
>
> What makes it non-accidental cannot lie *within* the world, since if it did it would itself be accidental.
>
> It must lie outside the world.
>
> 6.42 So too it is impossible for there to be propositions of ethics.
>
> Propositions can express nothing that is higher.

It is clear also that Wittgenstein would have said the same about the propositions of religion:

> 6.432 *How* things are in the world is a matter of complete indifference for what is higher. God does not reveal himself *in* the world.

Religion, ethics and aesthetics are concerned with expressions of *value*. They are *transcendental* in the sense that they 'lie outside the world', the sphere of contingent happenings.[37] They are inexpressible because they refer beyond the limits of the world, the sphere of significant expression.[38] We must not assume, however, that Wittgenstein is thus implying the existence of a super-factual domain for which ordinary language is inadequate, i.e., that there is a class of things which is 'inexpressible'—an ontological realm.

Many of the entries in Wittgenstein's *Notebooks 1914–1916* shed light on the *Tractatus* and several mention religion. Here are just a few examples:

> 11.6.16 The meaning of life, i.e., the meaning of the world, we can call God . . .
>
> To pray is to think about the meaning of life.
>
> I cannot bend the happenings of the world to my will: I am completely powerless.
>
> I can only make myself independent of the world—and so in a certain sense master it—by renouncing any influence on happenings.[39]

[37] *T.*, 6.41.
[38] See *T.*, 5.6: '*The limits of my language* mean the limits of my world.'
[39] *N.B. 1914–16*, p. 73.

Wittgenstein made the following entry about one month later:

> 8.7.16   To believe in a God means to understand the question about the meaning of life.
>
> To believe in a God means to see that the facts of the world are not the end of the matter.
>
> To believe in God means to see that life has a meaning.[40]

These entries do not, of course, show that the young Wittgenstein was himself religious. They do suggest, however, that when he thought of religion, he had in mind a special kind of affirmative attitude towards the inescapable facts and events of the world. Malcolm recalls an occasion when Wittgenstein had told him about the contempt he had for religion in his youth and how his attitude changed when he was about twenty-one years of age. 'In Vienna he saw a play that was mediocre drama, but in it one of the characters expressed the thought that no matter what happened in the world, nothing bad could happen to *him*—*he* was independent of fate and circumstances. Wittgenstein was struck by this stoic thought; for the first time he saw the possibility of religion.'[41]

The indifference of the religious attitude to '*how* things are in the world'[42] is clearly connected with the sayings about the mystical in the *Tractatus*. 'It is not *how* things are in the world,' says Wittgenstein, 'that is mystical, but *that* it exists.'[43] In conversation with Waismann, he directly links this expression to the religious attitude. They had been discussing religious language, and at one point Wittgenstein says: 'For me the facts are unimportant. But what men mean when they say that "*The world is there*" lies close to my heart.'[44] It is reasonable to conclude that the *religious* way

[40] Ibid., p. 74.
[41] *Memoir*, p. 70.
[42] T., 6.432.
[43] T., 6.44.
[44] *Philosophy Today*, No. 1, p. 19.

of wondering at the world and of making oneself independent of 'fate and circumstances' is very close to, though not
necessarily identical with, the 'mystical' in the *Tractatus*.[45]
Granted that there is this similarity, does it follow that
religious beliefs are ineffable in the same sense as that which
Wittgenstein called the mystical? It is difficult to give a
straightforward answer to this question. Could it be that
Wittgenstein meant that there could be no speech in religion
at all? This is hardly likely. Some years after the *Tractatus*,
in 1930, Wittgenstein said to Waismann that he could
imagine a religion in which nothing is said.[46] The answer to
our question is suggested by something Wittgenstein said
on that same occasion: '. . . if speech does occur, this itself
is a component of religious behaviour and not a theory.
Therefore nothing turns on whether the words are true,
false, or nonsensical.'[47] There could be genuine first-order
religious language according to the early Wittgenstein. What
he censures is 'theoretical' language which masquerades as
the language of religion. If there can be first-order religious
language, what then is *ineffable* about religion?

[45] It is perverse not to see the connection with religion when we consider
the following comments Russell made in a letter to Lady Otterline in
December, 1919, after a meeting with Wittgenstein: 'I had felt in his
book a flavour of mysticism, but was astonished when I found that he
has become a complete mystic. He reads people like Kierkegaard and
Angelus Silesius, and he seriously contemplates becoming a monk. It all
started from William James's *Varieties of Religious Experience*, and
grew (not unnaturally) during the winter he spent alone in Norway
before the war, when he was nearly mad. Then during the war a curious
thing happened. He went on duty to the town of Tarnov in Galicia, and
happened to come upon a bookshop, which, however, seemed to contain
nothing but picture postcards. However, he went inside and found that
it contained just one book: *Tolstoy on the Gospels*. He bought it merely
because there was no other. He read it and re-read it, and thenceforth
had it always with him, under fire and at all times. But on the whole he
likes Tolstoy less than Dostoewski (especially Karamazov). He has pene-
trated deep into mystical ways of thought and feeling, but I think
(though he wouldn't agree) that what he likes best in mysticism is its
power to make him stop thinking.' (Quoted in *Letters to Russell, Keynes
and Moore* (Blackwell, Oxford, 1974), p. 82).
[46] *Philosophy Today*, No. 1, p. 19.
[47] Ibid., p. 19.

Wittgenstein may well have thought that something 'ineffably' shows itself through the language of religion. It is not possible to discuss this question in detail, but it may be worthwhile glancing at the contents of a letter which Wittgenstein sent to Engelmann during the last stages of the work on the *Tractatus*. Engelmann had sent Uhland's poem, 'Count Eberhard's Hawthorn', to Wittgenstein in 1917. Wittgenstein replied as follows:

> The poem by Uhland is really magnificent. And this is how it is: if only you do not try to utter what is unutterable then *nothing* gets lost. But the unutterable will be—unutterably—*contained* in what has been uttered![48]

If something may ineffably 'show itself' through the language of poetry, we are probably justified in thinking that the same applies in the case of the language of religion. Religious language speaks for itself. It does not need to be supplemented or taken over by a theoretical or explanatory kind of language. There is something unutterably contained in what has been uttered. This is another way of saying that religion cannot be reduced to anything other than itself. The meaning of religion will be disclosed through religious behaviour and language. Whatever the difficulties that still surround the sense of the 'mystical',[49] Wittgenstein's claim that it *shows itself* may be meant to stress the *sui generis* character of religion, ethics and aesthetics.

There are two points to draw attention to before proceeding further. The first is that in the *Tractatus* statements about the value or the meaning of the world cannot be put in propositional form. I concluded that for the early

---

[48] Engelmann, pp. 7, 82–5.
[49] As W. D. Hudson argued in an unpublished essay ('Wittgenstein and the Mystical'), it is difficult to see how Wittgenstein's conclusions about the ineffable character of the mystical *follow from* his arguments about logical form. Both logical form and the mystical are supposed to *show themselves*. Granted the Picture theory of meaning, the way in which logic is transcendent is fairly clear. But how is the showing of logical form the same kind of thing as the showing of the mystical?

Wittgenstein, religious language was of this evaluative and non-theoretical kind. However, he suggests little more than this in his early writings. He did say more about the 'mystical', and this is the second point. I asked what follows if we link the 'mystical' in the *Tractatus* with religion. I concluded that, in spite of the ambiguities, Wittgenstein seems to censure any second-order, theoretical justification of religion. It will show itself. The 'itself' is as important as the 'show'. If a secondary medium comes in the way, religion itself may not be shown, just as an explanation of Uhland's poem may destroy its meaning. I mentioned in the Introduction that Engelmann believed that Wittgenstein's life and work offer the possibility of a new way of life. For Engelmann, the language of the new way—Wittgenstein's language—is what he calls the 'language of wordless faith.'[50] The exemplary lives will speak for themselves without the need of attempts to describe them. Whether we classify this kind of thinking as hopeless idealism or not, it is difficult to deny the direction and general tenor of Wittgenstein's influence upon Engelmann. It is a scepticism about the worth of any language which threatens the *sui generis* character of ethics, aesthetics and religion. By the time Engelmann came to give an assessment of the abiding importance of Wittgenstein, this scepticism had become very radical indeed: '. . . any doctrine uttered in words is the source of its own misconstruction by worshippers, disciples, and supporters.'[51]

Religion in the later period—Forms of Life and Language-games

Wittgenstein no doubt used these two terms to clarify his task of 'clearing up the ground of language.'[52] They have now become necessary jargon. The precise meanings of these terms is the source of great confusion. The problems

[50] Engelmann, p. 135.
[51] Ibid., p. 136.
[52] *P.I.*, 118.

are accentuated when we ask how they apply to religious belief.

Forms of Life

I shall be concerned with four main questions in what follows: (i) what did Wittgenstein mean by the term 'form of life'? (ii) what are the criteria for its application? (iii) how does it apply to religion? (iv) what precisely are the notions of justification, etc., which are closely related to this term? (i) Malcolm thinks it difficult to place too much stress on the importance of 'form of life'. If Malcolm is correct, both Wittgenstein and his interpreters have been guilty of unjustifiable silence on how a form of life is to be understood and identified. Malcolm himself is unhelpful. He gives the following as a good example of what Wittgenstein meant: 'The gestures, facial expressions, words, and activities that constitute pitying and comforting a person or a dog.'[53] Yet in his *Memoir* Malcolm expresses the belief that Wittgenstein looked on 'religion' as a form of life.[54] This may be so. But this means that the range of meaning is very wide. The example of pity and comfort could be regarded as a *feature* within the religious form of life. Yet, apparently, the larger whole to which pity and comfort belong is also a form of life.

There are several expressions in Wittgenstein's earlier works which seem to lie behind the concept of form of life as it eventually appears in the *Investigations*.[55] The whole point of using such expressions is to draw attention to the social contexts which give language its intelligibility. For example, consider the language-game of arithmetic: 'It is a concept,' says Wittgenstein, 'with a rigidly determined

---

[53] N. Malcolm, 'Wittgenstein's Philosophical Investigations' in G. Pitcher (ed.), *Wittgenstein: The Philosophical Investigations* (Macmillan: 1970 ed.), p. 91.

[54] *Memoir*, p. 72.

[55] See F. Zabeeh, 'On Language Games and Forms of Life' in E. D. Klemke (ed.), *Essays on Wittgenstein* (Univ. of Illinois Press, 1971), pp. 328–73.

activity in human life.'[56] As Wittgenstein comments in *Lectures and Conversations*: 'We don't start from certain words, but from certain occasions or activities.'[57] Some of Wittgenstein's early references to 'culture' seem to run parallel to his later references to form of life. In the *Investigations*, he says that 'to imagine a language means to imagine a form of life.'[58] And in *The Brown Book*:

> Imagine a use of language (a culture) in which there was a common name for green and red on the one hand and yellow and blue on the other . . .
>
> We could also easily imagine a language (and that means again a culture) in which there existed no common expression for light blue and dark blue.[59]

It is expressions such as 'culture', 'activities', 'whole life'[60] and the 'occasions' of use[61] which eventually crystallize into 'forms of life' in the *Investigations*.

Wittgenstein, in fact, uses 'form of life' only five times in the *Investigations*:

1. 'to imagine a language means to imagine a form of life' (*P.I.*, 19).
2. 'the *speaking* of language is part of an activity, or of a form of life' (*P.I.*, 23).
3. 'It is what human beings *say* that is true and false; and they agree in the *language* they use. That is not agreement in opinions but in form of life' (*P.I.*, 241).
4. 'the phenomena of hope are modes of this complicated form of life' (*P.I.*, p. 174).
5. 'What has to be accepted, the given, is—so one could say— *forms of life*' (*P.I.*, p. 226).

It is difficult to know precisely what Wittgenstein meant by form of life. Controversy still surrounds his use of this

---

56 R.F.M. V.35 186.
57 L.C., p. 3.
58 P.I., 19.
59 B.B.B., p. 134; see also L.C., p. 34.
60 B.B.B., p. 103.
61 L.C., p. 2.

term[62] and its application to religion.[63] Sherry, for example, thinks much depends upon whether religion is regarded as *a* form of life or whether it *contains* forms of life. He argues that by forms of life Wittgenstein meant 'basic human activities and responses like hoping, feeling certain, measuring, giving orders, asking questions, and greeting people, and indeed using language generally.'[64] On the basis of this definition, Sherry concludes that religion *contains* forms of life. He refers to the only example Wittgenstein gave of a form of life in the *Investigations*, and to an example mentioned in *On Certainty*. These are, respectively, 'hoping'[65] and 'feeling certain'.[66] It follows, according to Sherry, that their religious embodiments—Faith and Hope—are also forms of life contained *within* the many religious forms of life.[67]

There is an important issue at stake here because of the close connection between form of life and the question of justification in Wittgenstein. This issue will be discussed in more detail in relation to D. Z. Phillips' work. It may, however, be put crudely at this stage as a preparation for what follows. If religion is a form of life, then religious belief in its totality is 'the given' which must be 'accepted'.[68] That is, religion is not placed in a wider context of 'agreement',[69] and forced to justify itself according to the canons in that wider field. On the other hand, if religion *contains* forms of life in Sherry's sense, then they are particular expressions which can be located within the wider field of 'basic human activities and responses'[70] and may be called to account in

[62] E.g., J. F. M. Hunter, ' "Forms of Life" in Wittgenstein's *Philosophical Investigations*' *American Philosophical Quarterly*, Oct. 1968 Vol. 5 No. 4, pp. 233–43.
[63] P. J. Sherry, 'Is Religion a "Form of Life"?' *American Philosophical Quarterly*, April 1972 Vol. 9 No. 2, pp. 159–67.
[64] Ibid., p. 161.
[65] *P.I.*, p. 174.
[66] *O.C.*, 358.
[67] Op. cit., p. 162.
[68] *P.I.*, p. 226.
[69] *P.I.*, 241.
[70] Sherry, p. 161.

the name of some 'agreement' wider than that of religion. All of this is relevant to the question of whether there is an all-embracing concept of reality which I shall raise at a later stage.

'Form of life' as meaning a whole way of life should not be too readily dismissed. Janik and Toulmin provide much historical material which arguably supports this interpretation. They argue that since *Lebensformen* was a commonly used notion in Viennese intellectual circles of the 1920s, Wittgenstein could hardly have invented the term. Spranger's book on characterology, published just after the First World War, was widely read and had as its title, *Lebensformen*.[71] They note the significance of the friendship between Wittgenstein and Adolf Loos, the architect:

> . . . the notion of 'forms of life' as the contexts for the language games within which linguistic expressions acquire their meaning, is itself a strikingly Loosian notion. Loos himself had insisted that the design of any meaningful artifact must be determined by the 'forms of culture' within which it is used— the form of a chair by the way in which we sit, et cetera—so that changes in design have to be justified by changes in our manner of life, rather than vice versa[72].

To compress Janik's and Toulmin's discussion, they argue that Wittgenstein gave the existing notion of 'forms of life' an 'anthropological' dimension. In Viennese intellectual circles 'Lebensformen' were abstract schemata concerned with the categories and forms of thought. Wittgenstein stresses the *actual* features of human thought which provide the context for those categories.[73]

(ii) The question of *criteria* for identifying a form of life is, of course, closely related to how the idea is defined. Wittgen-

[71] *Wittgenstein's Vienna*, p. 230.
[72] Ibid., p. 230.
[73] Dallas M. High ('Belief, Falsification, and Wittgenstein'; *International Journal for Philosophy of Religion*, Winter 1972 Vol. 3 No. 4) p. 245, quoted from an unpublished manuscript to the effect that Wittgenstein wanted 'form of life' translated as 'way of living of human beings.'

stein himself provides no obvious criteria for its identification. If we attempt to identify forms of life by observing differences or disagreements between ways or modes of life, we are always confronted with a basic tautology. That is, if we say that certain differences (or disagreements) exist because they belong to different forms of life, we find that the differences themselves are the only criteria for determining the different forms of life. It is possible, of course, to draw up a list of things which seem to be constitutive for a particular way of life. For example, 'religion' is obviously—on a quite literal reading of form of life—one of the *forms* that life takes. Thus 'religion' may be phenomenologically identified, as Ninian Smart shows,[74] when he points to the various 'dimensions' of religion, namely, the ritual, mythological, doctrinal, ethical, social and experiential.

Wittgenstein offers no principles of selection, and his use of the term 'form of life' is weakened by the absence of examples. He may even have thought the request for principles of selection to be mistaken. We must be content with the advice to 'look and see' to discover whether there are ways of social life which may be described as forms of life in the sense that they are *distinguished* by certain practices and ideas.

(iii) The suggestion that religion is a form of life cannot be ruled out *a priori*, provided the religious way of life is acknowledged to overlap and be pervaded by features of social life which may be common to several different forms of life. I propose to discuss the question of how the notion of form of life applies to religion by studying D. Z. Phillips' work. For the moment I will consider certain important ideas which surround the idea and give it its importance in Wittgenstein's later work.

(iv) Wittgenstein did not use form of life as a simple quasi-sociological term. There are notions of justification closely related to it. A comment in *On Certainty* makes the point.

[74] *The Religious Experience of Mankind* (Fontana, 1971), pp. 15-25.

Now I would like to regard this certainty, not as something
akin to hastiness or superficiality, but as a form of life. . . .
But that means I want to conceive it as something that lies
beyond being justified or unjustified; as it were, as something
animal.[75]

Form of life here appears to be a further expression of the
recurrent theme in Wittgenstein: 'If I have exhausted the
justifications,' he argues, 'I have reached bedrock, and my
spade is turned. Then I am inclined to say: "This is simply
what I do." ';[76] and again, 'Our mistake is to look for an
explanation where we ought to look at what happens as a
"proto-phenomenon".'[77] Closely connected with this general
theme are Wittgenstein's references to 'culture',[78] 'natural
history'[79] and 'the common behaviour of mankind'.[80] In
short, Wittgenstein believes that there must be a point where
the giving of grounds and justification come to an end, but
'the end is not an ungrounded presupposition: it is an ungrounded way of acting.'[81] All these ideas are closely
parallel to an important reference to form of life in the
Investigations: 'What has to be accepted, the given, is—so
one could say—*forms of life*.'[82]

In their use of form of life Winch and Phillips have
assumed, as part of its intrinsic meaning, Wittgenstein's
rejection of demands for justification of something 'animal'
or 'given'. Consequently, Winch argues[83] that social behaviour is essentially meaningful because it is simply given.
Winch advises social scientists to look for *meaning* and not
cause. Social behaviour is given, part of the forms of life,

75 O.C., 358–9.
76 P.I., 217.
77 P.I., 654.
78 Z., 164.
79 P.I., 25.
80 P.I., 206.
81 O.C., 110.
82 P.I., p. 226.
83 P. Winch, *The Idea of a Social Science* (Routledge and Kegan Paul, London,
    1970 ed.).

and thus cannot but have meaning. Phillips has argued in a similar way about religious belief. The arguments of both Winch and Phillips have evoked considerable debate in their respective fields. Gellner in particular has attacked Winch's view.[84] However, Gellner's argument that forms of life do not always, or even frequently, accept *themselves* as given does not refute Winch's position. It is perfectly admissible on Wittgenstein's view that a form of life could reject its own past practices as absurd, irrational, etc.[85] The point is that practices cannot be rejected at will without presupposing a framework which makes alternatives intelligible.

Language-games

This notion, like that of forms of life, is ambiguous in Wittgenstein's writings. We are given no general theory of what a language-game is, nor how one is to be identified. Nevertheless, Wittgenstein does give many examples. In an important passage he provides a small catalogue of language-games, but before giving them he makes the following comment:

> . . . this multiplicity is not something fixed, given once for all; but new types of language, new language-games, as we may say, come into existence, and others become obsolete and get forgotten.[86]

If this is true it must be an important consideration in any attempt to relate language-games to religious beliefs. I will return to this issue later. For the moment we can notice that Wittgenstein's list includes 'Giving orders, and obeying them', 'Reporting an event', 'making up a story; and reading it', 'Asking, thanking, cursing, greeting, praying'.[87] 'The term "*language-game*",' says Wittgenstein, 'is meant to bring

---

[84] The most important criticisms are included in E. Gellner, *Cause and Meaning in the Social Sciences* (Routledge and Kegan Paul, London, 1973).
[85] See Gellner's comments, op. cit., p. 57.
[86] *P.I.*, 23.
[87] *P.I.*, 23.

into prominence the fact that the *speaking* of language is part of an activity, or of a form of life.'[88] If this quotation appears to resurrect all the ambiguity surrounding 'forms of life', the following comment may express his point more clearly: 'I shall also call the whole, consisting of language and the actions into which it is woven, the "language-game".'[89]

It is possible to extend the list of language-games in *Investigations* 23 by collecting together the many particular games mentioned throughout Wittgenstein's later writings; measuring with a metre-rule,[90] lying,[91] the activity of 'telling',[92] and of giving information,[93] etc. But how can we pick out an example of language and say, 'This is a language-game'? Indeed, how is a language-game related to what we understand by 'language' in the most general sense? Wittgenstein anticipates some of these questions at one point and acknowledges that he has nowhere said what the essence of a language-game is.[94] An objection might be framed as follows: 'So you let yourself off the very part of the investigation that once gave you yourself most headache, the part about the *general form of propositions* and of language.'[95] This reference back to the *Tractatus* points to one of the chief reasons behind his introduction of the idea of 'language-game'. His stress on the multiplicity of language-games is a fundamental part of his attempt to get rid of the assumption that logic is *prior to* all experience and that it constitutes the *a priori order of the world*. Logic is found *within* the various language-games themselves. That is, we learn to distinguish between sense and nonsense in different

---

[88] P.I., 23.
[89] P.I., 7; this recalls one of Wittgenstein's aphorisms recorded by Malcolm and later included in Z., 173: 'An expression has meaning only in the stream of life.' (*Memoir*, p. 93).
[90] P.I., 50.
[91] P.I., 249.
[92] P.I., 363.
[93] Z., 160.
[94] P.I., 65.
[95] P.I., 65.

ways by actually *using* language in the varied circumstances of social life.

In this light, we see that Wittgenstein's talk of language-games is not simply a colourful way of breaking up our everyday language into small, generalized compartments, e.g., asking, thanking, cursing, greeting, reporting an event, etc. Rather, it is to draw our attention to *the different shades of sense and nonsense* which may apply in different cases: 'We remain unconscious of the prodigious diversity of all the everyday language-games because the clothing of our language makes everything alike.'[96] However, in the absence of formal criteria, we can only assume that where the logic of a particular use of language marks it off from other uses, there we have a language-game. Nevertheless, we must take seriously Wittgenstein's references to family resemblances between games.[97] Wittgenstein says that a language-game 'is *not* closed by a frontier. For how is the concept of a game bounded? What still counts as a game and what no longer does? Can you give the boundary? No.'[98]

If forms of life are *given* so are language-games: '. . . the language-game is so to say something unpredictable. I mean: it is not based on grounds. It is not reasonable (or unreasonable). It is there—like our life.'[99] For example, Wittgenstein refers to the primitive language-game of teaching children to talk as being beyond justification.[100] 'Our mistake,' says Wittgenstein, 'is to look for an explanation where we ought to look at what happens as a "proto-phenomenon". That is, where we ought to have said: *this language-game is played*.'[101]

Before proceeding further I will attempt to clarify an issue which often befogs many discussions of this topic. We must

96   *P.I.*, p. 224.
97   *P.I.*, 66.
98   *P.I.*, 68; see also *P.I.*, 83–6, 499.
99   *O.C.*, 559.
100 *P.I.*, p. 200.
101 *P.I.*, 654.

not assume that, when Wittgenstein speaks of a language-game, he is necessarily associating it exclusively with *one* particular *practice* or *activity*. Rather, Wittgenstein is usually thinking of concepts which *run through* various activities without belonging solely to any particular kind of activity. It is true that the language *and* the associated behaviour make the concept intelligible, but we should not assume that a language-game will have an independent set of practices exclusively associated with it. Most of the language-games listed in *Investigations* 23 are not exclusively associated with particular practices. Asking, thanking, cursing and greeting may well be proto-phenomena, but they clearly *run through* all aspects of man's social, technical and religious life. Someone might thank God and another thank his lucky stars. But it is the concept of *thanking* which is the proto-phenomenon rather than any particular religious or astro-logical activity.

If these remarks are broadly correct, we cannot expect to discover the peculiar character of religious beliefs by concentrating solely on the concept of the language-game. We must look to Wittgenstein's idea of 'grammar', and the next chapter opens with an examination of this notion.

CHAPTER TWO

Grammar and the Sense of Religious Belief

THERE IS a series of letters in Bertrand Russell's auto-biography which discusses Wittgenstein's eligibility for a further research grant at Cambridge in 1930. Russell, through letters to G. E. Moore and a report to the Council of Trinity, comments on the new ideas in Wittgenstein's work since the *Tractatus*. Russell refers to Wittgenstein's 'peculiar' uses of the words 'space' and 'grammar'. In a letter to Moore on 5th May, 1930, Russell comments: 'One might define a "space", as he uses the word, as a complete set of possibilities of a given kind. If you can say "This is blue", there are a number of other things you can say significantly, namely, all the other colours.'[1] In his report to the Council Russell adds that 'Wittgenstein uses the word "grammar" to cover what corresponds in language to the existence of these various "spaces". Wherever a word denoting a region in a certain "space" occurs, the word denoting another region in that "space" can be substituted without producing nonsense, but a word denoting any region belonging to any other "space" cannot be substituted without bad grammar, i.e., nonsense.'[2]

During his 1930–33 lectures at Cambridge, Wittgenstein said that we should be using his 'jargon' if we thought that the sense of a sentence depended on 'whether or not it was constructed according to the rules of grammar.'[3] He some-times used 'grammar' in the straightforward sense of the

---

[1] *The Autobiography of Bertrand Russell* (Allen & Unwin, London, 1975 ed.), pp. 437–8.
[2] Ibid., p. 439.
[3] See G. E. Moore's report in his *Philosophical Papers* (Allen & Unwin, London, 1959), p. 276.

internal consistency of language, the parts of speech, etc. But I am concerned here with the 'peculiar' use which Wittgenstein made of the term. For example: 'One ought to ask, not what images are or what happens when one imagines anything, but how the word "imagination" is used. *But that does not mean that I want to talk only about words.*'[4] Indeed, he does not reject the tendency to ask about the essence of the thing itself. But in the paragraph which follows the last one quoted he says '*Essence* is expressed by grammar' and 'grammar tells what kind of object anything is (Theology as Grammar.).'[5]

The difference between the straightforward use and Wittgenstein's peculiar use of 'grammar' was probably in his mind when he distinguished between *surface* and *depth* grammar.[6] The grammar (or 'depth grammar') of a concept is its meaning or sense, i.e., what can and what cannot be said of it: 'I want to say the place of a word in grammar is its meaning.'[7] Take, for example, language-games concerned with colours. Propositions such as 'There are four primary colours', 'There is no colour between red and green', etc., are grammatical statements. They are rules which characterize the colour language-game or games. If we protest and argue that the above propositions simply express *truths* which derive from the *essence* of the colours in question, Wittgenstein reminds us that the recognition of particular colours presupposes not only sight, but also the framework of our language.[8] When we recognize or point to colours we are dependent upon an established way of speaking about colours. People understand our pointing, recognizing, etc., only if 'the overall role of the word in language is clear.'[9]

Wittgenstein's use of 'grammar' is inextricably bound up

4   *P.I.*, 370; my italics.
5   *P.I.*, 371 and 373 respectively.
6   *P.I.*, 664.
7   *P.G.*, p. 59.
8   See *Z.*, 332: 'Do not believe that you have the concept of colour within you because you look at a coloured object—however you look.'
9   *P.I.*, 30.

with our ways of reasoning, measuring, judging, etc. It applies to the way we speak about a word, an object, and also the fundamental features of human life. When Wittgenstein says that 'grammar tells what kind of object anything is', he is not concerned to relate the physical features of an object. The grammar of 'chair' establishes the *concept* of a chair in our whole system of concepts. It distinguishes the *way* one sits on a chair from, say, sitting on a cigarette. A chair can be broken, but not in the same way that clocks, homes or promises are broken.[10] But 'grammar' is also related to ways of thought as fundamental as those which assume the existence of the material world or the uniformity of nature. Wittgenstein makes the following comment about the philosopher's general concern with the problem of the relation of 'language' to 'reality': 'The connection between "language and reality" is made by definitions of words, and these belong to grammar, so that language remains self-contained and autonomous.'[11] Does this mean, according to Wittgenstein, that all metaphysical problems may be resolved by paying attention to 'grammar'? It seems so: 'Like everything metaphysical the harmony between thought and reality is to be found in the grammar of the language.'[12]

We might be tempted to ask about who *decides* upon the grammar appropriate to something. Is 'grammar', like 'forms of life', something which is simply 'given'? Wittgenstein said that 'a language-game is only possible if one trusts something.'[13] He appears to be saying that there is a certain unquestionableness about 'the *scaffolding* of our thoughts'[14] which constitutes the very possibility of our having frames of reference at all. Wittgenstein himself puts

[10] See H. F. Pitkin, *Wittgenstein and Justice* (University of California Press, 1972), pp. 117–19.
[11] *P.G.*, p. 97.
[12] *P.G.*, p. 162.
[13] *O.C.*, 509.
[14] *O.C.*, 211; see also 83.

into words the question which might occur to us in the light of this: ' ". . . So does it depend wholly on our grammar what will be called (logically) possible and what not,—i.e., what that grammar permits?"—But surely that is arbitrary! —Is it arbitrary?'[15] The question is whether the frames of reference within which one determines what is real and what is not are arbitrary. This is a vital question and some care is needed to follow Wittgenstein's reasoning here.

At one point he states that the rules of grammar are 'akin both to what is arbitrary and to what is non-arbitrary.'[16] A clue to the kind of distinction Wittgenstein draws is provided earlier in *Zettel*:

> One is tempted to justify rules of grammar by sentences like 'But there really are four primary colours'. And the saying that the rules of grammar are arbitrary is directed against the possibility of this justification, which is constructed on the model of justifying a sentence by pointing to what verifies it.[17]

Therefore, when Wittgenstein says that grammar is 'akin to what is arbitrary', he is asserting the nonsensicality of attempting to *justify* rules of grammar. It makes no sense to attempt a justification by comparing 'grammar' with a reality external to it.[18] The rules of grammar do not need *grounds* or *foundations* to legitimate them. The grammar itself gives *expression* to the grounds of our reasons, judgements, etc., in any particular context.

Nevertheless, there may be a further protest. Granted that the rules of grammar are not arbitrary as, say, the rules of ludo, are they not arbitrary in the sense that they are contingent upon the kind of facts of nature we experience? Wittgenstein anticipates this objection:

> If the formation of concepts can be explained by facts of nature, should we not be interested, not in grammar, but rather

15 *P.I.*, 520.
16 *Z.*, 358.
17 *Z.*, 331; see also *P.I.*, 497.
18 See *P.G.*, p. 186.

in that in nature which is the basis of grammar?—Our interest certainly includes the correspondence between concepts and very general facts of nature.[19]

But it is the *kind* of relation between 'grammar' and the 'general facts of nature' which rules out any charge of arbitrariness for Wittgenstein. The rules of grammar are concepts which we 'relax' into accepting. Children do not begin from scratch to decide the grammar appropriate to talk about material objects.[20] Unless we take some things for granted, we cannot make judgements at all. But it is the *way* in which these presuppositions enter into our lives which makes the charge of arbitrariness inappropriate. Our particular rules of grammar reflect the style of human life *and* the 'facts of nature' as we find them. The essential point is that the facts *alone* do not account for the concepts we have. Indeed, what we have come to regard as 'the facts' is dependent upon the techniques, ways of speaking, etc., which have made our life what it is.[21]

Dilman has put the point very concisely. Following Wittgenstein, he notes the way in which we accept certain grammatical propositions as 'unquestionable, indubitable, unassailable', and comments:

> That we regard *some* things in this way is part of speaking, reasoning and judging. *What* in particular we so regard is part of our natural history. It is *both* dependent on the kind of beings we are, the kind of environment in which we live, *and* also makes us the kind of beings we are. We do not *choose* what we are to regard as unassailable.[22]

We could say, for example, that measuring things is part of our natural history. A proposition like 'twelve inches equals one foot' is arbitrary, conventional. However, the *concept of measurement* is not arbitrary. Granted the kind of world we

---

[19] *P.I.*, p. 230.
[20] See *O.C.*, 472–3.
[21] See *P.I.*, p. 230.
[22] I. Dilman, *Induction and Deduction* (Blackwell, Oxford, 1973), p. 166.

have and the kind of beings we are, when we apply our concept of measurement we experience constant results.[23] If basic changes in the weight, size and shape of, say, lumps of cheese, were experienced, then both our concept of measurement and activities involving cheese would have to be different.[24]

We can perhaps best grasp the significance of all of this by remembering the view of language which pervaded Wittgenstein's later writings. Life and language are not two separate things. Language is not *added* to social life to facilitate communication, as though language were simply a *means* to express something apart from itself:

> Where does language get its significance? Can we say 'Without language we couldn't communicate with one another'? No. It's not like 'without the telephone we couldn't speak from Europe to America'. . . the concept of language *is contained in* the concept of communication.[25]

In the next section I shall draw attention to some of Wittgenstein's 'direct' references to religious belief. However, some readers may think already that Wittgenstein's ideas could not possibly apply to religion. This may have occurred to them in the discussion of language-games when we noted that Wittgenstein said that some language-games may become obsolete. This suspicion may also have been confirmed in the present section when I suggested that, on Wittgenstein's view, it does not make sense to justify 'grammar' with anything *external* to it. A natural reaction is to retort that whatever may be the case about any other aspect of human life, religious language-games, if there are such things, could never become 'obsolete'. Furthermore,

---

[23] *P.I.*, 242.

[24] *P.I.*, 142; see also *O.C.*, 63, 513, 558.

[25] *P.G.*, p. 193; see R. Rhees' essay, 'Could language be invented by a Robinson Crusoe?' in O. R. Jones (ed.) *The Private Language Argument* (Macmillan, 1971), pp. 61–75; 'The point is that no one could invent just *language*. Language goes with a way of living. An invented language would be a wallpaper pattern; nothing more.' (p. 69).

how could religious beliefs be anything other than fanciful uses of language if that language—and its 'grammar'—is not connected with a reality external to it? We shall see what such fears amount to later in the study.

Wittgenstein's Direct References to Religion

I have already mentioned the danger of thinking that Wittgenstein offers theories about religion when he appears to be referring directly to the topic. He never gave an exhaustive philosophical analysis of religious belief but there are a few shorter writings which have an obvious bearing on any discussion of Wittgenstein's view of the grammar of religious language. There are three main sources for these writings; (i) Wittgenstein's 'Remarks on Frazer's "Golden Bough" ' (1931 and c.1936);[26] (ii) *Lectures and Conversations on Aesthetics, Psychology and Religious Belief*; and (iii) isolated remarks in the later writings, the *Investigations*, *Zettel*, etc. In his notes on Wittgenstein's lectures 1930–33, G. E. Moore reports that Wittgenstein wanted to say something about the grammar of the expression 'God', but, in fact, said very little.[27] Moore's notes do not take us very far and I will confine myself here to the three sources mentioned above.

(i) *Remarks on Frazer's 'Golden Bough'—The Mythology in Our Language*

As Rhees warns us in his introduction to these 'Remarks', Wittgenstein is not writing directly about religion, or history and anthropology for that matter.[28] He is concerned with the mythology of our language: 'A whole mythology is

---

[26] *The Human World*, May 1971 No. 3, pp. 18–41 (with Introductory notes by R. Rhees).

[27] *Mind*, Jan. 1955, p. 16.

[28] Sees Rhees' introduction to R.F.G.B., p. 18; cf. N. Rudich & M. Stassen, 'Wittgenstein's Implied Anthropology: Remarks on Wittgenstein's Notes on Frazer' *History and Theory*, Vol. 10, No. 1 (1971), pp. 84–9.

deposited in our language.'[29] Frazer failed to see this. He did not recognize the basic kinship between the activities and language of primitive man and those of our own culture: 'too little is made of the fact that we include the words "soul" and "spirit" in our own civilized vocabulary. Compared with this, the fact that we do not believe our soul eats and drinks is a minor detail.'[30] A brief summary of Wittgenstein's remarks on Frazer may provide a good introduction into the spirit of Wittgenstein's treatment of religious belief in *Lectures and Conversations*. No attempt will be made to defend Frazer here.

(a) Frazer's observations are crudely ethnocentric. Where these are combined with explanations, the latter are much cruder than the primitive practices themselves.[31] Frazer's 'narrowness of spiritual life' makes him more savage than the so-called savages he studies.[32] He cannot understand a way of life different from the English one of his own time: 'Frazer cannot imagine a priest who is not basically an English parson of our times with all his stupidity and feebleness.'[33]

(b) Frazer's major mistake was his obsession with *explanations*. Wittgenstein does not believe that a culture-gap creates an unbridgeable disjunction between our world and the primitive's. The mythology is part of *our* language too. We do not need to construct a *theory* of ancient magic and ritual practices. Neither do we need to search for new facts to assist us in making hypotheses.[34] Frazer rightly saw that the death of the King of the Wood at Nemi was a very serious ceremony, but he trivialized his own insights by raising questions which invite *explanatory* answers. Something 'strange and terrible' *was* happening in the ceremony: 'And

[29] R.F.G.B., p. 35.
[30] R.F.G.B., p. 35.
[31] R.F.G.B., p. 34.
[32] R.F.G.B., pp. 31–2; 35.
[33] R.F.G.B., pp. 31–2.
[34] R.F.G.B., p. 30.

that is the answer to the question "why is this happening?":
Because it is terrible . . . Put that account of the King of the
Wood at Nemi together with the phrase "the majesty of
death", and you see that they are one. The life of the priest-
king shows what is meant by that phrase'.[35]

Wittgenstein's comments on the *Golden Bough* bring out
very sharply the sense in which he rejects reductionist
explanations of religious ceremonies. The practices are not
about bad scientific theories, and the participants are not
'stupid'.[36] The ceremonies only appear superstitious if we
neglect the role they play in people's lives. Consider the
practice which is sometimes called 'sympathetic magic':

> Burning in effigy. Kissing the picture of a loved one. This
> is obviously *not* based on a belief that it will have a definite
> effect on the object which the picture represents. It aims at
> some satisfaction and it achieves it. Or rather, it does not *aim*
> at anything; we act in this way and then feel satisfied.

> The same savage who, apparently in order to kill his enemy,
> sticks his knife through a picture of him, really does build his
> hut of wood and cuts his arrow with skill and not in effigy.[37]

These examples provide an illuminating background to
what Wittgenstein said in later years about the character of
Christian beliefs. We shall see later how he stresses the
absolute, non-hypothetical nature of these beliefs. We can
see here how strongly he resists the tendency to *explain*
beliefs and practices: ' . . . the explanation is too uncertain.
Every explanation is an hypothesis.'[38] The idea that primitive
man was awed by natural phenomena because he could *not*
explain them is a 'stupid superstition' of our time.[39]
(c) In attempting to explain religious practices, Frazer
thinks that the participants commit 'errors' or 'mistakes'.

35 R.F.G.B., p. 30.
36 R.F.G.B., p. 29.
37 R.F.G.B., p. 31.
38 R.F.G.B., p. 30.
39 R.F.G.B., p. 33.

Even where various religions express their differing traditions (e.g., Augustine and a Buddhist holy man),[40] it does not follow that some of them must be mistakes: '*none* of them was making a mistake except where he was putting forward a theory.'[41] We can speak of 'mistakes' or 'errors' only within the context of opinions, hypotheses and explanations.[42] This again anticipates some of the ideas in *Lectures and Conversations*.

(d) More positively, Wittgenstein thinks that the anthropologist should *describe* and not explain. Understanding is possible: 'when I read Frazer I keep wanting to say: All these processes, these changes of meaning,—we have them here still in our word-language.'[43] For example, the tradition of the priest-king: 'The religious actions of the religious life of the priest-king are not different in kind from any genuinely religious action today, say a confession of sins. This also can be "explained" (made clear) and cannot be explained.'[44] We can only *describe*, says Wittgenstein, and say 'human life is like that.'[45] Thus, to summarize, for the Wittgenstein writing in the early 1930s, there was an expressive language still surviving in everyday language which points towards a truer understanding of primitive man's beliefs and practices. Is there such a 'mythology' in contemporary uses of language? I shall return to this and related issues in the final chapter.

(ii) *Lectures and Conversations on Aesthetics, Psychology and Religious Belief* (1938–1946)

These notes are fragmentary, often cryptic and very

---

[40] R.F.G.B., pp. 28–9.
[41] R.F.G.B., p. 29.
[42] R.F.G.B., p. 30.
[43] R.F.G.B., p. 36.
[44] R.F.G.B., pp. 30–1.
[45] R.F.G.B., p. 30. D. Z. Phillips contrasts Wittgenstein's approach with that of the early anthropologists in *Athronyddu Am Grefydd* (Gomer Press, 1974), pp. 27–30; 94–5; etc.

puzzling. W. D. Hudson finds them 'fascinating, suggestive, provocative',[46] yet Flew thinks them 'scrappy and generally inconclusive'.[47] Such contrasting reactions reflect differing philosophical expectations of the lectures. Nevertheless, left to speak for themselves, at least three themes emerge.

(a) Religious beliefs are *absolutes* rather than hypotheses or opinions: ' . . . one would be reluctant to say: "These people vigorously hold the opinion (or view) that there is a Last Judgement". "Opinion" sounds queer . . . We don't talk about hypothesis, or about high probability. Nor about knowing.'[48] The 'total' character of belief is not a consequence of good evidence, however indubitable: 'Because the indubitability wouldn't be enough to make me change my whole life.'[49] Indeed, the absolute nature of a religious belief *shows* itself by the way in which it regulates all of the believer's life.[50] The absolute, necessary character of religious beliefs is parallel in some sense to Moore's necessary propositions which Wittgenstein discusses in *On Certainty*:

> I do not explicitly learn the propositions that stand fast for me. I can *discover* them subsequently like the axis around which a body rotates. This axis is not fixed in the sense that anything holds it fast, but the movement around it determines its immobility.[51]

Very closely related to this is a passage in which Wittgenstein comments on the way a child learns to accept some things as unshakeably fast: 'Children do not learn that books exist, that armchairs exist, etc., etc.—they learn to fetch books, sit in armchairs, etc., etc.'[52] It is only later that questions about the *existence* of things arise (e.g., 'Is there such a thing as a

---

46 'Some Remarks on Wittgenstein's Account of Religious Belief' G. Vesey, et. al. *Talk of God* (Macmillan, London, 1969), p. 36.
47 *Spectator*, Sept. 16th, 1966, p. 355.
48 L.C., p. 57.
49 L.C., p. 57.
50 L.C., p. 54.
51 O.C., 152.
52 O.C., 476.

unicorn?'). Up till then the existence of books and chairs, etc., was taken for granted.[53]

(b) The 'firmness' of religious beliefs is perhaps best described by relating it to another theme of *Lectures and Conversations*, 'pictures'. The believer's 'pictures' constitute the *framework* for what it makes sense to say of his experience of life. A picture might play the role of moral constraint: 'the role of constantly admonishing me.'[54] To doubt the truth of this is not strictly to *disagree* with the believer.[55] The kind of disagreement between believer and unbeliever is so fundamental that their disagreement cannot be located *within* any mode of discourse:

> I think differently, in a different way. I say different things to myself. I have different pictures.
>
> It is this way: if someone said: 'Wittgenstein, you don't take illness as punishment, so what do you believe?'—I'd say: 'I don't have any thoughts of punishment.'[56]

There is a similarity here again between what Wittgenstein says about religious belief and what he says in *On Certainty* about the necessary proposition that I have two hands: 'What would I believe if I didn't believe that? So far I have no system at all within which this doubt might exist. I have arrived at the rock bottom of my convictions.'[57]

It is because the belief or 'picture' is an all-regulating framework that it is not tentatively or hypothetically held. It is an absolute, 'rock bottom' conviction in the sense that it constitutes what it makes sense to say of his life. The picture is not absolute because it is like a spindle which is held fast by something else. It is like an axis which is 'held fast by what lies around it';[58] i.e., what a believer does and

[53] 'What stands fast does so, not because it is intrinsically obvious or convincing; it is rather held fast by what lies around it' (*O.C.*, 144).
[54] *L.C.*, p. 56.
[55] See *L.C.*, p. 55.
[56] *L.C.*, p. 55.
[57] *O.C.*, 247–8.
[58] *O.C.*, 144.

says about his life. In some ways 'picture' is a misleading word to use in talking about religious belief. It suggests that religious beliefs may be *representations* of something, or even that they may be *substitutes for* the real thing. These and other ambiguities will be discussed in the next chapter. We can simply note here that Wittgenstein did not think that pictures were convenient substitutes for something else: 'The whole *weight* may be in the picture.'[59]

(c) If Wittgenstein is correct in seeing religious belief in this way, it follows that the 'truth' of religious beliefs is *sui generis*; i.e., beliefs cannot be susceptible to the verifying and justifying procedures which apply outside the religious framework. As we have seen, for Wittgenstein, religious beliefs are not *true* in the sense that they are propositions based on good evidence. Expressions of belief are not used in the same way as hypotheses in science or history.[60] To say that believers and unbelievers are divided about the reliability of certain evidence is to mis-state completely the nature of the difference between them.[61] Where religious beliefs *are* held to be scientifically reasonable, they are 'unreasonable' and 'superstitious'.[62] Religious truth, so misconceived, appears as a 'blunder' out of its 'home' system. It strays into a foreign system or 'game'[63] where scientific reasonableness rules: 'If the question arises as to the existence of a god or God, it plays an entirely different role to that of the existence of any person or object I ever heard of.'[64] To speak of the 'truth' of religious beliefs, then, is to say that one lives by them, that they constitute the framework for one's life.

This account of the contents of *Lectures and Conversations* has been cursory by intention. All of the themes discussed

---

[59] *L.C.*, p. 72.
[60] *L.C.*, p. 57.
[61] See *L.C.*, pp. 53, 57, 58, etc.
[62] E.g., the view of Father O'Hara; *L.C.*, pp. 57–9.
[63] *L.C.*, p. 59.
[64] *L.C.*, p. 59.

briefly here will recur in the detailed discussion of D. Z. Phillips' work. There is little explicit use by Wittgenstein in the lectures of the ideas of forms of life and language-games. He does, however, say that one form of life may culminate in an utterance of belief in a Last Judgement.[65] What he says about the fact that religious beliefs are not 'blunders' may well depend upon his notion of language-games: 'Whether a thing is a blunder or not—it is a blunder in a particular system. Just as something is a *blunder in a particular game* and not in another.'[66]

(iii) *'Theology as Grammar'*

In the later literature there are two references to theology:

(a) *Essence* is expressed by grammar.

  Grammar tells what kind of object anything is. (Theology as Grammar).[67]

(b) How words are understood is not told by words alone. (Theology.)[68]

W. D. Hudson offers a few expository comments to the effect that 'Theology stands to religious belief . . . as its grammar does to a language.'[69] It is necessary, however, to go beyond this and relate 'grammar' to the peculiar term 'essence'. When Wittgenstein uses the word 'essence', he refers to the conventions in social and linguistic activities, seen as a single weave, e.g. 'If you talk about *essence*—you are merely noting a convention.'[70] These conventions are the *bedrock*, the *given*. As we saw earlier in the discussion of grammar, language is closely interwoven with the ways we view the world and our activities within it. The *given* or

---

[65] L.C., p. 58.
[66] L.C., p. 59; my italics.
[67] P.I., 371 & 373.
[68] Z., 144.
[69] *Ludwig Wittgenstein* (Lutterworth, London, 1968), p. 58.
[70] R.F.M., p. 23; see also P.I., 92; Z., 444, etc.

bedrock are formed through the grammar of our language. It is what people *do and say* which forms their grammar, i.e., what it makes sense to say is inextricably bound-up with what it makes sense to do.

The quotation from *Zettel* 144 ('How words are understood is not told by words alone. (Theology.)') is more intelligible in this light. Theology gives *expression* to a particular way of life. Words alone are empty of life. They have to be nourished by their use in a community. The language of religion has—or should have—an active grammar. The conventions (the essences) have made religion what it is. These essences are 'expressed by grammar'— grammar tells us 'what kind of object anything is.'[71] Nevertheless, we must not read too much into Wittgenstein's aphoristic remarks about theology. It seems reasonable to assume, however, that Wittgenstein's correlation of *grammar* and *essence* implies that theology must be related to a living community which embodies the conventions and beliefs expressed by theology.[72] Theology, as 'grammar', articulates the standards of intelligibility implicit in the language and activities of a religious tradition.

The early and later views—the thrust against the edges of language and the trespass of internal boundaries

At this stage some readers may fear that the substantive 'God' has been found as superfluous to religious language as, in earlier sections, *any* extra-linguistic Reality was superfluous to language in general. The fear may be based on a natural tendency to agree that whilst ordinary language *may* not need some sure connection with an external reality,

---

[71] *P.I.*, 373.
[72] R. H. Bell (*Theology As Grammar*, unpublished dissertation, Yale University Ph.D. 1968) discusses the consequences for the study of theology of Wittgenstein's point here, especially chaps. 7 and 8. See also Bell's 'Wittgenstein and Descriptive Theology' *Religious Studies*, Oct. 1969, Vol. 5 No. 1, pp. 1–18.

religious language *must* have this connection with its extra-linguistic subject, God, Spirit, Heaven, Hell, etc. Indeed, some might ask whether there is not a means, within the Wittgensteinian scheme, of making an exception in the case of religion. That is, the idea that the object of religious language comes in precisely where ordinary language runs out, i.e., at the edges or 'limits' of language. Let us see what this amounts to.

In Wittgenstein's early period, the *limits of language* is a technical idea. The limit of language is a single sweeping line enclosing all factual language and dividing sense from nonsense. It is located *a priori*. One could know when the dividing line had been reached and stop before straying into nonsense. In the *Investigations* Wittgenstein is less interested in the far-out boundary enclosing all discourse and concentrates on the boundaries *between* areas of discourse. The later Wittgenstein radically re-drew his map of language. Factual discourse is deprived of its pre-eminence and placed on the same level as all other modes. In the later period there is not a single boundary but a whole range, a maze of boundaries. These are determined, not *a priori*, but experimentally by a process of oscillation. In the *Tractatus*, nonsense appeared by the crossing of the external boundary. In the *Investigations* nonsense is produced by crossing an internal boundary without crossing it completely. The most familar example of this in the *Investigations* is the line between language about material objects and that of sensations.[73] The nonsense is produced by *straddling* the line, i.e., sensations are seen as objects, not material objects, but *mental objects*.

Is there a counterpart in the *Investigations* to the external boundary of the *Tractatus*? In the later work, the transcendental subjects of religion, ethics, etc., were taken in from what is sometimes called the 'penumbral' region into which they had been placed in the *Tractatus*. Indeed, religion appears to be a form or forms of life alongside other forms

[73]   *P.I.*, p. 180, etc.

of life, containing activities verbalized in language-games. One may ask whether *particular* forms of life are, by definition, still concerned with the distinction underlying the whole possibility of language. For example, is the religious form of life that which, by its very nature, operates at the limits of language, i.e., the point where the language of factual discourse is made to function in a way which makes it appear 'stretched' or even 'nonsense'? When a religious believer claims that God is a mystery or beyond human understanding, he is also claiming that language has *limits*. The question here is whether the all-encompassing boundary around factual discourse in the *Tractatus* becomes a major line through the religious mode of discourse. The issues are very complex here, but we can say a few things to clarify the relationship between Wittgenstein's earlier and later work.

I argued earlier that the transcendental subjects in the *Tractatus* are not ineffable because they refer to an ontological realm. It is unlikely, to say the least, that Wittgenstein thought that a religious form of life, or family of language-games, could be distinguished by its preoccupation with super-facts, which are *inexpressible* in straightforward factual language. If this is so, religious beliefs about the mystery or unknowability of God are not epistemological theories for Wittgenstein, in either his earlier or later philosophy. There may, of course, be distinctively *religious* ideas about the mystery of God which make a distinction between the effable and the ineffable. But this distinction, in the later period, is a *religious* one and is not equivalent to the earlier distinction between the all-encompassing line around factual language and nonsense beyond. In short, where it is still necessary to draw a distinction between the effable and the ineffable, it must be understood as it is actually drawn in, for example, the religious form of life.[74]

---

[74] Peter Winch, *Ethics and Action* (Routledge and Kegan Paul, London, 1972), p. 126, and D. Z. Phillips, *The Concept of Prayer* (Routledge and Kegan Paul, London, 1965), p. 40.

A recent study by Paul van Buren claims to be a working out of the implications of the *Investigations* for religious discourse. His thesis is that religious statements are made at the 'edges' of language, away from the safe, 'central plains' of language (scientific discourse, etc.)[75] He provides no argument to show how talk of such a far-out boundary of all language may be derived from the *Investigations*. The idea of a *standard* use of language (safe on the 'central plains'), factual, picturing discourse, is an idea from the *Tractatus* which Wittgenstein abandons in the *Investigations*. By suggesting that there is a safe, standard use of language, van Buren goes against the whole tenor of the *Investigations*. We cannot impose Wittgenstein's earlier concept of language on the later one, as van Buren appears to do. But can we not ask what becomes of Wittgenstein's great admiration for the ethico-religious tendency of running against the limits of language which he clearly had at some stage in his early period? In his 'Lecture on Ethics' Wittgenstein said, 'My whole tendency and I believe the tendency of all men who ever tried to write or talk Ethics or Religion was to run against the boundaries of language.'[76]

In the early period this urge to go beyond significant language produced a 'nonsensicality' which was of its 'very essence'.[77] He strongly resisted the idea that factual language could express the value, or sense of the world. To do so would be to compromise the *distinctive* character of religious beliefs, ethics, etc. Men still express wonder at the world, etc., but in the later period this is not a thrust against any 'outer' boundary of language. Where such 'metaphysical' expressions are uttered—to use the later terms—through religious forms of life, they may cross *internal* boundaries.

[75] Paul van Buren, *The Edges of Language* (S.C.M., London, 1972), esp. chap. 5.
[76] *Philosophy Today*, No. 1, p. 13. This lecture was prepared between Sept. 1929 and Dec. 1930. See also Wittgenstein's conversation with Waismann, 30th Dec. 1929, *Philosophy Today*, No. 1, p. 15.
[77] *Philosophy Today*, No. 1, p. 13.

However, this is not something which constitutes their 'very essence', as it did in the earlier period. Rather, if these trespasses are not detected, the very essence of their status as *religious* expressions is threatened, i.e., if they are confused with non-religious modes of discourse. Thus, although it is expressed in different ways, Wittgenstein's insistence upon the *sui generis* character of religious beliefs is as strong in *Lectures and Conversations* as it was in the *Tractatus*. Therefore, Wittgenstein's earlier respect for the tendency to run against the edges of language has a rough parallel in his later respect for genuinely *religious* expressions, which is evident in his insistence that religious beliefs are not metaphysical systems, pseudo-factual propositions or epistemological theories.

We could say, therefore, that the tendency Wittgenstein admired is better expressed in the later period as the urge to ask metaphysical questions. To describe Wittgenstein as an anti-metaphysician could create the wrong impression. He did not think that metaphysical questions are foolish. They arise from *deep* tendencies in our language:

> The problems arising through a misinterpretation of our forms of language have the character of *depth*. They are deep disquietudes; their roots are as deep in us as the forms of our language and their significance is as great as the importance of our language.[78]

Confusion arises if we look for *foundations* in order to resolve our metaphysical questions. Any attempt to discover an indubitable connection between language and reality is confused according to Wittgenstein. His own method is 'to bring words back from their metaphysical to their everyday use.'[79] When we pay attention to the 'apparently unimportant details of the particular situation'[80] we may see the confusion involved in trying to discover a framework to reality with which our language connects. The tendency to

[78] P.I., 111.
[79] P.I., 116.
[80] B.B.B., p. 66.

suppose that there is such a framework is one of the *deep* roots in language. In the next chapter I shall examine the work of a philosopher who has applied Wittgenstein's method very radically to religious belief.

CHAPTER THREE

Neo-Wittgensteinian Developments

PROFESSOR D. Z. PHILLIPS of Swansea, more than any other philosopher,[1] has consciously developed Wittgenstein's views in the field of the philosophy of religion.[2] Phillips' interest in Wittgenstein appears to stem directly from the influence of Rush Rhees, one of Wittgenstein's own students. Rhees' shorter writings[3] provide what is probably the best brief guide to what Phillips is pursuing. Picking up the legacy of his teacher, Rhees stresses the need to appreciate the peculiar *grammar* involved in language about God. One passage in particular conveys Rhees' own views on the character of that grammar and, incidentally, summarizes much of Phillips' work. It is worth quoting in full:

'God exists' is not a statement of fact. You might say also that it is not in the indicative mood. It is a confession—or expression—of faith. . . .

If you ask, 'Well, when we are talking about God, does our language not *refer* to anything?', then I should want to begin, as I have tried to here, by emphasizing something of the special grammar of this language. Otherwise it is natural to think of the way in which our physical object language may refer to something. The physical object language may not refer to anything either—if someone has made a mistake, for instance, or if the language is confused. And you might think that this is what I meant if I said that the language about God

---

[1] The writings of Paul L. Holmer of Yale are very deeply influenced by Wittgenstein. P. Sherry ('Learning how to be Religious' *Theology*, Feb. 1974, p. 84) considers Holmer's work to be the best attempt yet to relate Wittgenstein's philosophy to religion. I do not share this view, but I will not argue the point here.

[2] See bibliography for Phillips' writings.

[3] *Without Answers* (Routledge and Kegan Paul, London, 1969), esp. 'Natural Theology' (pp. 110–14), and 'Religion and Language' (pp. 120–132).

does not refer to anything. Which is obviously not the point. Or you might think that I meant that the language about God was just a sort of beautiful pretence; or perhaps that it was just part of the formality of a ceremony, like after dinner speeches. I do not mean anything of the sort, of course, and if I wanted to avoid *that* I might say that the language about God certainly does refer to something. But then I should want to say something about what it is to 'talk about God', and how different this is from talking about the moon or talking about our new house or talking about the Queen. How different the 'talking about' is, I mean. That is a difference in grammar.[4]

For Rhees it is grammatically confused to think that the language of religion is comparable to language which describes matters of fact.[5] Rather, religious language is *expressive* and *confessional*.[6] Thus, the *meaning* of religious belief is given in the kind of language believers use. The *language* of love, for example, is language used in a particular way: 'The sense of his 'I love you' is bound up with so much else in his life now. It is only on that account that it does mean anything. For I repeat, it is not saying that anything has happened, and it is not describing anything. Nor is it the expression of a sensation or feeling. It is the expression of love.'[7] Rhees argues, similarly, that it is the *language* of religion which makes a difference to what are, from one point of view, human practices, expressions of praise, fear, etc.: 'Reverence and devotion and exaltation, for instance, would not be what they are without the language of them. But I am not suggesting that religion is like the love of man and woman in any other way. I do not think it is. And the difference will appear in their different uses of language too.'[8] Wittgenstein's influence is very obvious here. If we give up

---

[4] *Without Answers* pp. 131–2.
[5] Ibid., p. 120.
[6] See *F.P.E.*, pp. 102, 107; *C.P.*, p. 147, etc,
[7] Op. cit., p. 123. Ian Robinson (*The Survival of English* (C.U.P., 1973) chaps. 5 & 6) shows how the erosion of the reality of love can be traced through the erosion of its language.
[8] Ibid., p. 125.

the idea of looking for an external framework, we will find the meaning of religious language precisely *in the language*.

Much of Phillips' work exists in embryo in the shorter papers of Rhees. Two broad tasks for the philosopher of religion are implicitly assumed in Rhees' writings and worked out in greater detail in Phillips' work; namely (i) the need to give an account of the *grammar* of religious belief; and (ii) the necessity of bringing out the distinctive *content* of religious beliefs. These two themes run through Phillips' accounts of the concept of God, prayer, love, duty, death and immortality, etc.

Philosophy and Religion

There is a passage in the *Investigations* which can be regarded as a foundation text for Phillips' programme of work:

> A philosophical problem has the form:
> 'I don't know my way about'.
> Philosophy may in no way interfere with the actual use of language; it can in the end only describe it.
> For it cannot give it any foundation either.
> It leaves everything as it is.[9]

This is the great relief offered to distraught flies! Phillips' attempt to administer the anodyne to his own particular fly— philosophy of religion—brings him into conflict with two commonly held views of getting through the wrong end of the bottle, namely (i) the idea that philosophy should provide some general argument for either the acceptance or rejection of religion; and (ii) the belief that the meaningfulness of religious statements may be tested by a general theory which provides a set of criteria for determining the significance or otherwise of such statements.

Phillips himself regards his own work as a new direction

---

[9] *P.I.*, 123–4; see *C.P.*, p. 1.

in contemporary philosophy of religion.[10] Whereas many philosophers of religion often begin by relating their own contribution to Flew's Falsification challenge of the 1950s, Phillips' position represents a vigorous rejection of the whole framework of that particular discussion. Ideally, as Phillips acknowledges,[11] for his own challenge to be established there should be a *prolegomenon* to the philosophy of religion which shows the diversity of criteria of rationality, i.e., 'whether there is any such thing as an all-embracing concept of reality, and to inquire whether the distinction between the real and the unreal comes to the same thing in every context of language.'[12]

To expand on points (i) and (ii): (i) The job of philosophy is to *elucidate* or *understand* religion, but not to evaluate or advocate: 'After it has sought to clarify the grammar of . . . beliefs its work is over.'[13] The task of clarification, following Wittgenstein, involves distinguishing between *surface* and *depth* grammar.[14] In more general terms, philosophy involves a study of the logic of belief and the implications which may be drawn. Phillips claims that philosophers have under-estimated the difficulties involved.[15] They have a 'craving for generality' which makes them guilty of 'arbitrary linguistic legislation'.[16] Philosophy must leave everything as it is. However, the situation may be changed for an *individual* whose awareness is changed through philosophy. He may be attracted or repelled. In either case it is not the concern of philosophy. (ii) Phillips challenges the idea of applying criteria which are at home in one context, e.g., that of

---

10 Hence the title of his most recent book: *Athronyddu am Grefydd; Cyfeiriadau Newydd* (Philosophizing About Religion: New Directions) (Gomer Press, 1974), see esp. pp. 9–10; cf. *C.P.*, p. 29.,

11 *R.U.*, p. 4.

12 *R.U.*, p. 4.

13 *F.P.E.*, p. 109.

14 *F.P.E.*, p. 131.

15 *F.P.E.*, p. 19; *R.U.*, p. 3; cf. *C.P.*, p. 158.

16 *F.P.E.*, p. 63. See *B.B.B.*, p. 17f. for Wittgenstein's analysis of what a craving for generality may involve in philosophical problems.

experimental science, to disciplines within which they are inappropriate. The notion of 'existence' may be unproblematic in one sphere. If the same concept is transferred *simpliciter* to the sphere of religious belief, we have an instance of an 'alien grammar' being introduced.[17] Phillips' claims have far-reaching consequences, if they are justified. They have often been misunderstood, and I shall discuss a few confusions briefly in an attempt to lay bare the brunt of Phillips' position.

It is often assumed that Phillips thinks that it is impossible to *understand* religious claims without *believing* them.[18] Ninian Smart, for example, mentions one of the results of Wittgenstein's influence in conversation with Bryan Magee:

> *Smart*: . . . That is the use of certain ideas and hints in Wittgenstein to evolve a philosophy of religion which implies that you have to believe in order to understand, so that religion is either true or meaningless. I am thinking in particular of the work of D. Z. Phillips in his *The Concept of Prayer* and some of his other writings . . . But I am personally not altogether favourable to this approach, because it would put me out of a job, or least out of half a job, since it would make the study of religions other than one's own, presumably—(*pause*)
> *Magee*:—a waste of time?
> *Smart*: A waste of time . . .[19]

Smart misunderstands Phillips' position here. It is natural theologians and a certain kind of apologist who face redundancy. Philosophers of religion are guaranteed employment on Phillips' view.

One of the hints Smart may have in mind is where

---

[17] See *C.P.*, p. 81, and cf. Wittgenstein's comment: 'If the question arises as to the existence of a god or God, it plays an entirely different role to that of the existence of any person or object I ever heard of.' (*L.C.*, p. 59).

[18] E.g. T. Kasachkoff, 'Talk about God's Existence' *Philosophical Studies* (The National University of Ireland) 1970, Vol. XIX, p. 183; H. Palmer, 'Understanding First' *Theology*, March 1968 Vol. LXXI No. 573, pp. 107–114; etc.

[19] *Modern British Philosophy* (Paladin Books, 1973), p. 214.

Wittgenstein argues that it is impossible to contradict a person who expresses a belief in a Judgement Day:

> In one sense, I understand all he says—the English words 'God', 'separate', etc. I understand. I could say: 'I don't believe in this,' and this would be true, meaning I haven't got these thoughts or anything that hangs together with them. But not that I could contradict the thing.
>
> You might say: 'Well, if you can't contradict him, that means you don't understand him. If you did understand him, then you might.' That again is Greek to me. My normal technique of language leaves me. I don't know whether to say they understand one another or not.[20]

Wittgenstein's reluctance in the final sentence is due to his fear of misleading people, if they take 'understand' in too straightforward a sense. Wittgenstein does not mean that the believer and unbeliever do not understand one another at all. In one sense, an unbeliever does understand and, in another, he does not. Take the experience of falling in love. Is it possible to understand this experience if one has never fallen in love oneself? Lovers often say that one has to be in love really to appreciate what love is, and those still waiting for the experience usually take the point. But in another sense, the non-participant does understand what love is. He has learned to recognize when people are in love, and he knows that he will not be completely baffled if the experience comes his way.

There is no dogmatic identification of belief and understanding in Wittgenstein's writings, and it is difficult to see why his general position should entail this. It is also difficult to see how Phillips' development of Wittgenstein should result in such an identification. As Phillips says, 'One can know the moves in chess without having a love for the game.'[21] Phillips does also retain the sense in which the unbeliever does *not* understand the believer. He stresses that

[20] *L.C.*, p. 55.
[21] *C.P.*, p. 83; cf. *F.P.E.*, p. 221.

there can be no *theoretical* knowledge of God, and at one point quotes Malcolm's words: ' "belief in God involves some affective state or attitude" '.[22] Malcolm is obviously correct in this, but it does not prevent a sympathetic outsider from having 'some feeling for the game'.[23] Phillips' position fully allows for this possibility.

Let me take up a further point of confusion. Phillips constantly stresses that the function of philosophy in relation to religion is to provide a conceptual analysis of its content. *Advocacy* is outside the philosopher's brief.[24] But is Phillips' own philosophy as 'pure' as he implies? This question is bound to arise when we realize that throughout his writings he advocates a concept of *true religion*.[25] It will become clear later just what this concept is. As one would expect, Phillips does not attempt to give reasons for his concept of true religion in accordance with an external norm. Faced with religious phenomena as divergent as early Hebrew barbaric practices and the passion of Christ, Phillips is in no doubt which of these embodies genuine religion.[26] A truly religious belief is one which is consistent with God considered as an *absolute reality*, a belief which is itself held to be of *absolute worth*. This is a religious point. A good philosophical analysis preserves true belief intact by elucidating its grammar. Phillips' work is directed against theologians and philosophers who conceive God as a *relative* reality—making Him a 'fact' at some point along a broader common measure which deals with matters of fact. They make faith a *conditional* rather than an *absolute* value.

The 'advocacy' at the heart of Phillips' work is his assumption that the absolute reality of God and worth of faith can only be preserved and properly analysed philosophically in expressive and non-factual terms. He seems to

<hr/>

22 F.P.E., p. 32.
23 C.P., p. 83.
24 F.P.E., pp. 72–3; C.P., pp. 23, 29, 106.
25 E.g., R.U., p. 6; *Saith Ysgrif ar Grefydd*, p. 134, etc.
26 R.U., p. 6.

assume that the second is a necessary corollary of the first. This is to state the matter very baldly. There is a highly complex relationship between the two in Phillips' writings. The concept of genuine religion is a major determining factor in all that Phillips says about the nonsensicality of subjecting religion to external criteria of rationality. In other words, Phillips is not *simply* saying, with Wittgenstein, 'Philosophy must leave everything as it is'; he is arguing for a particular view of *what*, in fact, should be left as it is. He does not begin with a general thesis about the impossibility of judging religion externally. Rather, the *kind* of religious belief determines whether or not it is to be understood solely in terms of internal criteria or be subjected to 'external' standards. I put *external* in inverted commas because if a belief does not express genuine religion, it is already explicable in terms of non-religious modes of discourse which are externally related to religion. For example, if certain eschatological beliefs are understood in a factual, future sense, then there is no question, on Phillips' view, of these beliefs being elucidated only by internal criteria. As *factual* beliefs, whether expressed through a religious vocabulary or not, they are subject to the standards prevailing in the mode of discourse which deals in matters of fact. These eschatological beliefs are *not* left 'as they are'; they are indirectly classified as suspect religion. If a genuine religious belief is expressed philosophically in factual terms, then this must be classified as suspect philosophy.[27]

If it is taken as a general theory (that religion cannot be assessed by external criteria), one can easily see how sceptical philosophers might challenge Phillips' thesis, namely, on the grounds that the criteria for understanding religious beliefs are closely related to so-called 'external standards'. The sceptical philosopher may be opposing the 'internal criteria only' argument on the assumption that the religious

[27] See *F.P.E.*, pp. 266ff.

beliefs had some *factual* reference. Faced with Phillips' insistence that beliefs have no such reference, the sceptical philosopher could then reply that he now has no reason to oppose Phillips' 'internal criteria only' argument. The disagreement between Phillips and the sceptics would then centre upon the issue of the essential character of religious belief, upon what is genuine religion and the right method of philosophical analysis.

It is sometimes thought that Phillips' work is an attempt to *protect* religion.[28] However, Phillips' insistence that the criteria of intelligibility are internal to religion does not guarantee that any possible answer is favourable to religion: 'On the contrary, my thesis is as necessary in explaining unbelief as it is in explaining belief.'[29] Atheism and agnosticism are certainly not ruled out in Phillips' philosophy; they are simply understood in the same non-factual, expressive sense as religious belief itself. On this view, atheism is the recognition 'that religion means nothing to one'.[30]

In summary, most people would probably agree that it makes no sense to make a blanket assertion about the meaninglessness of religion in general. But might not certain religions—indeed, all but *one* religion—be mistaken? This is a convenient point to comment on the question of different religions in the Wittgensteinian approach. My comments will be brief because I do not think that the problems are as great as, say, Ninian Smart believes them to be for the Wittgensteinian view. There are, of course, many very complex questions of truth in view of the existence of many religions, but this is not the point I am making here. Smart thinks that to use a language-game approach somehow isolates one religion from the opposing truth-claims of other

---

[28] Ninian Smart speaks of Phillips' effort to make religion intellectually respectable again—see chaps. 5 and 6 of *The Science of Religion and the Sociology of Knowledge* (Princeton University Press, 1973). See also C. W. K. Mundle's *A Critique of Linguistic Philosophy* (Clarendon Press, Oxford, 1970), p. 249.

[29] F.P.E., p. 12.

[30] C.P., p. 19; see also pp. 20, 106; F.P.E., p. 68.

religions.[31] But why should this be so? Phillips is objecting to the idea that *philosophy* could decide between religions. Philosophy might help to distinguish religion from superstition but this is another matter. It would be an interesting exercise to see how the Wittgensteinian approach applied in detail to religions other than Christianity, but this is outside the scope of the present book.

Forms of Life and Language-games

Phillips does not argue in detail for applying these concepts to religion. He assumes them, together with the other characteristically Wittgensteinian stress on grammar and use, as the tools for his philosophical work of analysis. Phillips, like Wittgenstein, appears to ask whether amongst the vast inter-relatedness of all aspects of social life and language, there are beliefs, practices, uses of language, etc., which 'resemble' each other in such a way that full justice is not done to them if they are not seen to belong to a larger whole. Such larger wholes are marked by agreement in certain basic presuppositions. These conditions are arguably what Wittgenstein meant by a form of life. I have already mentioned Wittgenstein's answer to anyone who retorted, 'So you are saying that human agreement decides what is true and what is false?'; which was, 'It is what human beings *say* that is true and false; and they agree in the *language* they use. That is not agreement in opinions but in form of life.'[32] Particular opinions within a form of life may be right or wrong, but the agreement on the criteria for saying so is given in the form of life.

When Phillips employs the language-game approach in the philosophy of religion and analyses the distinctive language-games of religion, it is important to grasp the precise nature of what he is claiming. He is *not* implying,

[31]   See chap. 5, *The Science of Religion and the Sociology of Knowledge.*
[32]   *P.I.*, 241.

for example, that religious worship is cut off from everything outside the formalities of worship. This would be an absurd claim and would make religion a fantastic, esoteric game.[33] However, Phillips does refer to the *distinctive* language-game of religious belief.[34] Is he making the mistake of associating language-games exclusively with a particular set of practices? It is difficult to give a straightforward answer. I will attempt to clarify the issue by means of examples. Let us take one of the language-games which Wittgenstein includes in his catalogue of games in the *Investigations*,[35] namely, that of 'forming and testing a hypothesis'. It is fairly clear that this cannot be exclusively associated with a particular practice or set of practices. It is true that the practice of science most easily comes to mind, but there is no limit to the number of circumstances in which one could speak of forming and testing a hypothesis across the whole spectrum of social life. I might form the hypothesis that my friend is at this moment staying at a particular house and test it by going to see. No practice could then claim to be *distinctive* on the grounds that forming and testing a hypothesis is exclusive to it. It is a concept which *runs through* many practices.

If someone claimed that religious beliefs are types of hypotheses which will eventually be tested, say, eschatologically, then they are not distinctive in so far as they resemble other kinds of beliefs we call hypotheses. Phillips' point is that religious beliefs are not hypotheses. As a hypothesis, the belief in a Last Judgement would be thought of as a future event which might or might not occur: 'Those who feel sure it will occur, those who think it might possibly occur, and those who do not think it will occur are all, logically, on the same level. They are all playing the same game: they are expressing their belief, half-belief, or unbelief

---

[33] See *F.P.E.*, pp. 96–7.
[34] See *F.P.E.*, p. 101.
[35] *P.I.*, 23.

in a hypothesis.'[36] Similarly, how are we to regard the activities of a boxer crossing himself before a fight; a mother placing flowers on a statue of the Virgin Mary; parents praying for their lost child?[37] Phillips asks whether we are to regard these as blunders or religious activities. If they are beliefs which involve testable hypotheses, that is, if the mother thinks that the flowers are of prudential value, etc., then, according to Phillips, they are 'blunders' because they contradict what we know about casual connections.[38] He goes on to say that we need not understand them as hypotheses and, in fact, we distort religious beliefs by introducing the notion at all. The boxer may be dedicating himself; the mother may be thanking God for his gift of a child; the parents may be asking God that they be able to meet their loss in the awareness of his presence. 'The beliefs involved,' says Phillips, 'are not testable hypotheses, but ways of reacting to and meeting such situations. They are expressions of faith and trust.'[39]

This comment from Phillips presumably represents his way of showing how religious beliefs and practices, whilst not hypotheses, are nevertheless distinctive language-games. Yet the language-games of asking and thanking are present in at least two of the examples considered above. Asking and thanking[40] clearly run through many practices. Does Phillips imply that asking and thanking in those examples are nevertheless distinctive? We are beginning to see some of the difficulties in Phillips' claim that religious beliefs are *distinctive* language-games. Whatever the consequences may be for Phillips' general position, we are bound to say that he cannot avoid acknowledging that some language-games (e.g., 'thanking' and 'asking') run through many practices, *including religion*, but that certain language-games

36   F.P.E., p. 88.
37   F.P.E., p. 101.
38   F.P.E., p. 102.
39   F.P.E., p. 102.
40   See Wittgenstein's list in P.I., 23.

(forming and testing a hypothesis) cannot be part of the framework of religious belief if the latter is to be recognized for what it essentially is.

This difficulty need not be insurmountable for Phillips. He could argue that the normal practices of asking and thanking resemble the religious concepts of asking and thanking sufficiently for them to be regarded as belonging to the same 'family'. Clearly, on Phillips' view, forming and testing a hypothesis does not belong to the same family of language-games that constitute religious belief. To summarize, therefore, we could say that Phillips' own application of the language-game approach involves the belief that language-games run through many and varied practices, including religion, but that there are some games which must be expressly excluded from religion. Phillips' approach depends, of course, on what he has made of the other vital Wittgensteinian themes such as 'grammar' and 'pictures'.

The Truth of Religious 'Pictures'

For Phillips, religious belief represents a total disposition towards the world. This disposition is focused for the believer in certain 'pictures'. The commitment to these is *total*, and the believer does not argue for the truth of them as he may do for the truth of empirical assertions. Rather, they constitute what counts as truth for the believer. He does not measure their adequacy against a broader notion of truth; he is measured by them.[41] Yet it is possible to speak of the 'truth' of religious beliefs and Phillips frequently does so.[42] From this point of view, there is something inappropriate about asking *why* people have certain religious beliefs. It is like asking why people have certain moral values; one can only reply that they do, that is all:[43] 'The values are adhered

[41] *D.I.*, p. 77
[42] See *D.I.*, p. 71.
[43] See Phillips' Introduction to J. L. Stocks, *Morality and Purpose* (Routledge and Kegan Paul, London, 1969), p. 4.

to for their own sakes, because they are what they are.'[44]
Neither belief nor loss of belief is determined by the evidence in Phillips' view. That is, a believer's mind is not changed by a new estimate of the evidence. Phillips speaks of a loss of belief in the Last Judgement and comments that where this happens 'the *attention* of the individual has been won over either by a rival secular picture, or, of course, by worldliness, etc. Because his energies are now focused in another direction, this picture which was once powerful in his life, has lost its grip.'[45] The question begged by all of this is, of course, what are these 'pictures' which are so powerful and all-regulating? What sense is being ascribed to 'picture'? It is obviously related to Wittgenstein's use of the term. However, much of the contemporary discussion of this concept is both confusing and, I will argue, confused.[46] For example, Nielsen argues that the use of the term 'picture' connotes some notion of *representation*, i.e., 'there must be something which the picture is a picture of'.[47] Nielsen therefore concludes that any notion of 'picture', such as Phillips' use, which rules out any understanding of 'this "something that is pictured" ', is incoherent and obscure.[48]

Unlike Nielsen, Hudson has offered a sympathetic treatment of the idea of 'picture' as this was used in *Lectures and Conversations*. Nevertheless, Hudson's interpretation seems incompatible with Phillips' use of the notion. Hudson argues that when 'religious belief is spoken of as "using a picture",

---

[44] Ibid., p. 10. Phillips' Introduction reveals very clearly how he has been influenced by Stocks' opposition to the interpretation of moral values in terms of purposive action, or to giving justifications for them in non-moral terms, and this is echoed in many of Phillips' essays in the philosophy of morals and religion.

[45] *F.P.E.*, p. 116.

[46] See W. D. Hudson, 'Some Remarks on Wittgenstein's Account of Religious Belief': ' "Using a Picture" and Religious Belief', *Sophia*, July 1973 Vol. XII No. 2, pp. 11–17; K. Nielsen, *Scepticism* (Macmillan, London, 1973), chap. 2; M. Durrant, *The Logical Status of 'God'* (Macmillan, London, 1973) chap. 4; 'The Use of "Pictures" in Religious Belief' *Sophia*, July 1971 Vol. X No. 2, pp. 16–21.

[47] *Scepticism*, p. 36.

[48] Ibid., p. 36.

the word "picture" in this expression obviously means a mental picture of some sort as distinct from the kind of object which is hanging on the wall before me as I write.'[49] Some of Wittgenstein's references to 'picture' clearly refer to the notion in the sense of a *mental image*. However, I will argue below that this is not the sense in which Phillips has developed the term.

Durrant's discussion is the most detailed criticism yet of Phillips' idea of 'pictures'. Indeed, Durrant claims that Wittgenstein's own use involved a basic misunderstanding which both Phillips and Hudson have carried over uncritically into their own interpretations. Durrant argues that Wittgenstein was mistaken in assuming (i) that words *represent* and (ii) that some sentences can be regarded *as* 'pictures'.[50] Durrant himself assumes that Wittgenstein's position depends upon the notion that words and sentences have a representational function in a similar way to that performed by signs in the vocabulary of art.[51] Durrant concludes that we can only make sense of Wittgenstein's and Phillips' usage if we ignore their assumptions that some sentences *express* pictures or are pictorial representations, and concentrate on the fact that sentences may nevertheless *present* us with certain pictures.[52]

Much of Durrant's criticism is beside the point because it dwells too much upon the *representational* sense of 'picture'. Like Nielsen, Durrant asks how it is possible to say that the religious 'picture' expresses something if we can give no independent account of what is being expressed.[53] He asks for the *decision procedures* involved in saying that a certain 'picture' has a particular role and concludes that Phillips provides us with none.[54]

---

[49] ' "Using a Picture" and Religious Belief', p. 11.
[50] *The Logical Status of 'God'*, pp. 86ff.
[51] Ibid., pp. 88–90.
[52] Ibid., pp. 92–3.
[53] Ibid., p. 97.
[54] Ibid., p. 95.

The critics of Phillips' religious 'pictures' have not been sensitive enough to the possible levels of meaning in the notion. Nielsen and Durrant have concentrated on the use of 'picture' in the sense of *something corresponding to an object*. Hudson has based his development of Wittgenstein's suggestions mainly on 'picture' as a *mental image*. All three writers neglect the all-important notion of *grammar* in Wittgenstein's thought. This is the aspect which Phillips appears to stress, but his presentation of the idea has been very ambiguous. To clarify the matter, I will break down Wittgenstein's use of 'picture' into three senses, all of which are arguably present in *Lectures and Conversations*.

(i) 'Picture' as *something which corresponds to an object*: this particular sense of picture is found throughout Wittgenstein's writings and is used in the quite straightforward sense of painting, photograph, diagram, projection, puzzle-picture, etc.[55] This is the sense of 'picture' in *Lectures and Conversations* when Wittgenstein refers to pictures of aunts,[56] of biblical subjects,[57] of tropical plants,[58] etc., and where there is a well-recognized 'technique of comparison' relating the visual image to the reality. The examples I have just mentioned were given by Wittgenstein in order to draw a contrast between those pictures (and the accompanying techniques of comparison), and pictures of God: 'But not the same consequences as with pictures of aunts. I wasn't shown (that which the picture pictured)'.[59]

There is an ambiguity in Wittgenstein's discussion which may have caused confusion over what he meant by *religious* pictures. He refers to Michelangelo's painting of God creating Adam and says that someone could grasp what was meant by a picture of a tropical plant, even though that person had never seen the plant in question: 'There is a

[55] *P.I.*, 280; Z., 231–3, etc.
[56] *L.C.*, p. 59.
[57] *L.C.*, p. 63.
[58] *L.C.*, p. 63.
[59] *L.C.*, p. 59.

technique of comparison between picture and plant'.[60] By contrast, to show someone Michelangelo's painting and say ' "Of course, I can't show you the real thing, only the picture" ' would be absurd, if I had not also taught him the technique of using the picture.[61] The ambiguity arises from the fact that, in Wittgenstein's example, both the picture of the plant and that of God are *visual* images, implying that although the technique of comparison for God is different from that appropriate to aunts and plants, it is nevertheless *representational* in some sense. But Wittgenstein's choice of a religious 'picture' here was probably unfortunate. A religious training does not usually involve *visual* images to represent God in such an anthropomorphic way. It was, perhaps, Wittgenstein's discussion here which caused some sceptical philosophers to insist that the religious 'picture' represents something, and has encouraged more sympathetic philosophers to emphasize the 'picture' as a mental image.

(ii) 'Picture' as *mental image*: there is also a wide use of this sense of 'picture' in Wittgenstein's work.[62] There are a few comments in *Lectures and Conversations* which could possibly be taken in this sense. Hudson, for example, argues that it is this sense of 'picture' which lies behind a comment like the following: 'Suppose somebody made this guidance for this life: believing in the Last Judgement. Whenever he does anything, this is before his mind';[63] or in the following: 'suppose we said that a certain picture might play the role of constantly admonishing me, or I always think of it.'[64]

(iii) 'Picture' as the *logical space* of a belief: 'When I say he's using a picture I'm merely making a *grammatical* remark: (What I say) can only be verified by the consequences he does or does not draw.'[65] This is the sense of 'picture' which

[60] L.C., p. 63.
[61] L.C., p. 63.
[62] E.g. P.I., 139–40; Z., 238–46, etc.
[63] L.C., p. 53.
[64] L.C., p. 56.
[65] L.C., p. 72.

has been neglected by Durrant, Nielsen and Hudson and which appears to dominate Phillips' analysis of religious belief. Strangely enough, this use of 'picture' seems to be related to the notion of the *proposition* as a picture in the *Tractatus*: 'A picture presents a situation in logical space.'[66] There are, of course, equally obvious differences which appear when such a quotation is set within Wittgenstein's earlier theory of language. For example, 'In order to tell whether a picture is true or false,' says Wittgenstein, 'we must compare it with reality.'[67] Such a notion is incompatible with Wittgenstein's later use of 'picture'. 'Picture' in this third sense is in no way concerned with the sense of something corresponding to an object, whether this be a visual image before one's eyes or a mental image in the head. Rather it is the framework, the space, or logical space in which sense and nonsense can be spoken, the limits within which sense and nonsense have their reference. This sense of 'picture' reminds us of the connection Russell noted between 'grammar' and 'space' when commenting on Wittgenstein's work in 1930.[68] As we have seen, Russell believed that 'space' in Wittgenstein's work of that period was used for a 'complete set of possibilities of a given kind'.[69] To confuse logically different 'spaces' was to be guilty of 'bad grammar'.

I suggest, therefore, that we should have these kind of considerations in mind when Wittgenstein links 'pictures' and religious beliefs, rather than any *representational* sense, be it of the visual or mental kind. Thus, a religious 'picture' may be thought of as a framework containing a complete set of possibilities, some of which may be explicit and others implicit. The 'grammar' of the 'picture' would determine the implications to be drawn. For example, to believe in a Last Judgement would not be to contemplate a future

[66] *T.*, 2.11.
[67] *T.*, 2.223.
[68] See p. 41.
[69] *The Autobiography of Bertrand Russell*, pp. 437–8.

event of a particular kind. The language of *prediction* is a 'possibility' excluded from that particular 'picture'. It would be to encroach upon another 'space' and be guilty of bad grammar. For it to be a *religious* belief, it would have to have —as a matter of 'grammar'—an *absolute* character. It could only have this character if it was not contigent upon an event which may happen in the future. The *Last* Judgement, from a Wittgensteinian view of the grammar of belief, is 'last', not as the final event in a lifelong series of events, but a *final*, permanent, eternal scrutiny which is always present in the midst of contingent judgements. It is the framework enclosing all of the believer's thoughts and actions, not an assessment at the *end* of his earthly life. The sense of *absolute* here would be part of the grammar of any religious picture we care to mention, in the sense that belief cannot be contingent upon the way things go in the world or outside the world. It is not uncommon today to hear even theologians saying that there can be no religious absolutes in our day. According to the Wittgensteinian view I have been discussing, when religious beliefs cease to have an absolute character, they cease to be *religious* beliefs. The word 'absolute', of course, refers to the integrity of the believer's values and not the certainty that something is 'there'.[70]

I have tried to show, therefore, that a 'picture' conceived as a logical space is closely related to what Wittgenstein says in *Lectures and Conversations* about the grammar of religious belief. This is evident, I think, when he talks about the impossibility of *contradicting* a believer, because one is not involved in the same mode of discourse. That is, the *framework* for the believer's commitment is different from the unbeliever's: 'I think differently, in a different way. I say different things to myself. I have different pictures.'[71] Thus

[70] Peter Winch develops this sense of absolute in relation to the willing of the Good in the work of Socrates, Wittgenstein and Kierkegaard; see *Ethics and Action* (Routledge and Kegan Paul, London, 1972), pp. 193–209.

[71] *L.C.*, p. 55.

when Nielsen asks about the logic of what the picture *corresponds to*, or when Durrant asks about the *decision procedures for* the pictures, the answers implied by Wittgenstein's general position (as I have outlined it) are intelligible even if open to challenge. Thus, whether a belief corresponds to something, or what is to count as making a decision, are themselves determined by the logical space within which they are raised. The logic of the correspondence is determined by the grammar of the picture in question; a decision is always a decision of a particular kind, namely, that defined by the framework to which the believer is committed. If this third meaning of 'picture' is taken as primary in *Lectures and Conversations*, then Wittgenstein's comments to the effect that 'he has it constantly before his mind' or 'he always thinks of it', which Hudson interprets as referring to mental images, could mean that *this whole way of thinking* is constantly before his mind; that is, it sets limits to what he believes about God and defines the grammar of its content. The pictures are the *means* rather than the object of assessment.[72] They are the diamonds which cut everything else.

In the past two decades there has been no shortage of short-hand terms to characterize the framework of commitment of religious belief. The offers range from 'bliks', 'onlooks', 'end-statements', to 'paradigms' and 'metaphysical systems'. We can now add 'pictures' to this list. All of the terms mentioned are, of course, theory-laden. To use them is to work on the assumption that religious belief is to be understood in a particular way. The question which concerns us here is what are the assumptions about the nature of religious belief which accompany talk of 'pictures'?

The Existence of God and the Reality of Genuine Religion

Some readers may think that the best way of answering the last question is to ask, aside from all the talk of 'pictures',

[72] See *D.I.*, p. 72; *F.P.E.* p. 90, 118, etc.

'grammar', etc., whether 'God' exists in the neo-Wittgen-steinian scheme. This suggestion is, of course, less straight-forward than it sounds. However, for the sake of clarifying Phillips' position we can allow the question to stand; 'Does God exist?' Three things are worth saying about this.

(a) Phillips is uneasy with the form of the question itself, particularly when it is asked with a view to 'finding out'.[73] His unease is acute if the quest for an answer is in the terms of philosophical detachment. He asks, 'What would it be like for a philosopher to settle the question of the existence of God?'[74] Phillips thinks that many philosophers crudely impose the grammar of another mode of discourse on religion, namely, that appropriate to the existence of physical objects.[75] Their mistake is to think that they could under-stand what a 'purely theoretical' belief in the existence of God would be like.[76] Phillips is happier if the question is one asking about the *reality* of God. In this case, it is possible to answer by saying that such a question is about a *kind of reality* and not about the reality of *this* or *that* as in a question concerning physical objects. Whatever else it means, coming to believe that there is a God is something involving much more than an extension of one's knowledge. Rather, it 'involves seeing a new meaning in one's life, and being given a new understanding.'[77] Granted this, what of the answer to the question 'Does God exist?' Is it then the case that it can be answered internally?

(b) Phillips would presumably answer 'No' to this question. It cannot be answered within the sphere of re-ligious discourse because the real 'existence' of God is always a presupposition within that particular form of life. God is a reality in the religious language-game or set of games. Thus any talk of the 'existence' of God could only be in terms of

[73] *F.P.E.*, p. 131; *C.P.*, p. 60.
[74] *F.P.E.*, p. 14.
[75] *F.P.E.*, p. 132.
[76] *F.P.E.*, p. 14.
[77] *F.P.E.*, p. 18.

the propriety of such a term granted the *kind of reality* God has. That is, 'existence' (of God) would be debated in terms of whether it accorded with the good *grammar* of the subject. Phillips would probably say that the usual usage of 'to exist' makes its application to 'God' extremely hazardous. To say that something exists may imply that it could eventually cease to exist. Believers, of course, would never say that God might cease to exist. They think in this way, not because as a matter of fact God will exist for ever, but because it makes no sense to say that God might cease to exist.[78]

(c) It follows, also, from Phillips' view that the question cannot be answered within any *other* form of life. The word 'real' is a context-dependent notion. Thus the reality of God's existence will be treated differently in areas of discourse different from the religious one. Consequently, any other universe of discourse will misunderstand the question. It is only 'at home' in the religious one, and even there it has to be treated with great care. The chief difficulty of talking about the *existence* of Phillips' God is that the term 'God' does not describe anything on his view. It is not a *name* of someone or something. The word 'God' derives its meaning from within the complex patterns of religious reactions to the contingency of the world. To discover what kind of reality this 'God' has we must pay attention to those religious reactions. I will glance briefly at one such religious reaction, the language of Eternal Life, to the supreme contingency—death. But first I will comment on Phillips' idea of the *independent* existence of God and then on the notion of genuine religion.

The Independent Existence of God

In the light of Phillips' analysis, a question could be raised about the independent existence of God in a time when no one acknowledged his reality. For example, Trigg asks: 'Are those who have lost all religious belief at fault

[78]   F.P.E., pp. 85-6.

in that they are ignoring what is true . . . ?'[79] Phillips does not think it contradictory to speak of a time when no one acknowledged God:

> . . . religious believers can say something *now, from within the picture*, about such a time of radical absence of belief. What they say is not that God has died, but that in such a time, people have turned their backs on God.[80]

During the time of radical absence of belief, God would play no part in anyone's religious picture, and thus, for Phillips, it can only make sense to speak of such a period now, i.e., while there are believers with pictures. Therefore, even in the hypothetical case of a future absence of belief, Phillips resolutely refuses to attempt to speak of the *independent* existence of God. He is only prepared to speak of an *independent* reality in the sense of the following:

> . . . In learning by contemplation, attention, renunciation, what forgiving, thanking, loving, etc., mean in these contexts, the believer is participating in the reality of God; *this is what we mean by God's reality.*
>
> This reality is independent of any given believer, but its independence is not the independence of a separate biography. It is independent of the believer in that the believer measures his life against it.[81]

Phillips makes essentially the same point in *The Concept of Prayer*: '. . . understand what is meant by His divinity, and you understand what is meant by His existence at the same time.'[82] When these differences are ignored, the issue is removed from the domain of religion where alone it has its meaning. In a period of total unbelief that domain would be absent.[83] At one point Phillips goes so far as to say that there

---

[79] R. Trigg, *Reason and Commitment* (C.U.P., Cambridge, 1973), p. 90.
[80] *D.I.*, p. 78: my italics.
[81] *D.I.*, p. 55.
[82] *C.P.*, p. 38.
[83] Phillips' essay, 'From World to God?' (*F.P.E.*, pp. 35–61) includes a discussion of the sense of speaking of the *independent* existence of God, and I will mention this later in the study.

will be no progress in the philosophy of religion until we realize that the reality of God is the same as His divinity.[84] In spite of what I have said so far, many readers of Phillips' works will no doubt still be puzzled about the precise nature of divine reality Phillips has in mind. If we follow the hints contained in his essays we will find an answer by taking account of the *eternity* of God.[85] Probably the best source material for filling in the portrait of Phillips' Eternal God are the writings of Kierkegaard, and particularly his *Purity of Heart*[86] on Man and the Eternal.

Kierkegaard talks of 'Eternity's Emissaries to Man', namely, remorse, repentance and confession.[87] To experience these is to hear the 'voice of eternity'. This God has no location, yet is ever-present[88] and timeless. He is present in the form of His emissaries. The 'voice of eternity' 'speaks' through Huckleberry Finn's *confession*, when he realizes for the first time that 'You can't pray a lie'.[89] The same voice is heard through the death-bed *repentance* and *remorse* experienced by Tolstoy's Ivan Ilych. It is not possible here to expand upon Kierkegaard's subtle and profound account of the Eternal's dealings with man. We can simply notice at this stage that it is such a concept which lies behind Phillips' often unexplained references to the eternity of God.

Genuine Religion

I mentioned earlier that Phillips' idea of 'true religion' is vital to an adequate understanding of his work. He provides no systematic account of this idea, but he acknowledges on occasions that his philosophical accounts presuppose an idea

---

[84] *Athronyddu am Grefydd*, p. 13.
[85] E.g., *C.P.*, p. 82.
[86] Fontana Books, 1961.
[87] Ibid., pp. 34–46.
[88] D. Z. Phillips says at one point that he does not deny that *presences* are felt or that voices are heard in religious experiences (*C.P.*, p. 136). However, the implication of his whole position is that such presences and voices could not be related to the Eternal God he has in mind.
[89] See P. Winch, *Ethics and Action*, p. 196.

of what genuine religion is.[90] Phillips' defence against the charge that his notion of true religion is an arbitrary one is that his work attempts to justify his choice by bringing out the actual roles that beliefs play in people's lives. Thus 'My idea of what prayer is must be justified by showing how it takes account of the complex behaviour of religious believers in various situations.'[91]

At the heart of Phillips' conception of a genuine religious belief lies the distinction between the *eternal* and the *temporal*. The temporal is concerned with the transient and changeable things of our earthly life. But what is the eternal? Summarizing Phillips' work very briefly, the eternal is that which never changes, namely, the life of God. A believer can only enjoy eternal life himself by participating in God's life. But how is this possible? The religious answer is, 'Through grace'; that is, through the Spirit of God. Grace is given to the believer as he enters into a particular relationship with the world and with other people.[92] In Phillips' view it is Simone Weil who has provided the best treatment of grace,[93] and this accounts for the numerous references to her ideas in his essays. In view of the importance of the 'eternal' and 'grace' to Phillips' estimate of genuine religion, I will glance briefly at one aspect of Simone Weil's thought which has so impressed him.

The value of the eternal is grasped only if we have died to the world's way of regarding things. For example, there is one aspect of the spirit of man which is at odds with the eternal view, namely, the deeply felt, natural right for compensation.[94] The spirit of man demands equal pay. If a man expends energy in doing good or suffers hurt by being wronged, he expects compensation. We enjoy life and health

---

[90] *C.P.*, p. 158; *R.U.*, p. 6.
[91] *C.P.*, p. 158.
[92] See *Saith Ysgrif ar Grefydd*, p. 131.
[93] Ibid., p. 131.
[94] See Simone Weil *Gravity and Grace* (Routledge and Kegan Paul, London, 1963), pp. 5–9.

as possessions which are naturally ours. Illness and death threaten these rights. We *feel* the need for compensation even though this may never come. By contrast, the believer views *everything* as a gift. He has died to the longing for compensation. He has died, in fact, to the self. This is the 'daily death' necessary for every Christian.[95] In *The Concept of Prayer* Phillips quoted a passage from *The Sickness Unto Death* (Kierkegaard) as central to his whole thesis: '. . . God *is* that all things are possible, and that all things are possible *is* God.'[96] This is a very puzzling statement but it becomes intelligible in the context of what I have just said. To believe that everything is possible with God is not, for the true religious believer, to believe that God will make everything right for him in the end, or that God can do *anything*. From the eternal view, whatever the world may regard as *essentials* are, for the believer, only *possibilities*. For him everything is a gift; nothing is his by right. All things are merely possible. No circumstance, thing, etc., is *essential* to a believer who looks at life in this way. They are possibilities which may or may not come to be. Nothing in fact depends upon whether they actually come to be.

This brief excursion into Phillips' idea of genuine belief is not of merely incidental interest. On the contrary, his estimate of what is true religion determines what kind of philosophical analysis is required. There are, of course, many alternatives to Phillips' idea of what religious belief is supposed to be about. Bertrand Russell had a very different idea in mind in his lifelong insistence that theological beliefs should not be accepted unless there is the same kind of evidence for them as is demanded for scientific propositions.[97] Some believers accept this stipulation, but, unlike Russell, they believe that there is evidence for God. Phillips' point is that the *very idea* of evidence is out of place

---

[95] See *Saith Ysgrif ar Grefydd*, p. 134.
[96] *C.P.*, p. 129.
[97] *The Autobiography of Bertrand Russell*, p. 36.

in religious belief. It is not that the evidence is of a particularly subtle and illusive kind. As Wittgenstein put it: 'The point is that if there were evidence, this would in fact destroy the whole business.'[98] Russell once said that if he were brought before his Maker, he would ask why the Almighty had provided so little evidence of His existence. Speaking from within the Wittgensteinian tradition, Dilman comments[99] that Russell betrayed a complete incomprehension of spiritual matters.

Death and Eternal Life

We can see the radical difference between the eternal and the temporal in Phillips' treatment of death and eternal life.[100] There is a way of speaking of immortality in *temporal* terms. Miguel de Unamuno expresses his 'hunger for immortality': 'I dread the idea of having to tear myself away from my flesh . . . if I grapple myself to God with all my powers and all my senses, it is that He may carry me in His arms beyond death . . . Self-illusion? Talk not to me of illusion—let me live!'[101] In an early essay,[102] Phillips acknowledges the force of the natural longing for life to continue and admits at that stage that he did not know whether there was room for a continuation of life in the concept of Eternal Life. In later essays it is obvious that he excludes any idea of such a continuation. Indeed, Phillips warns against the tendency some of his readers might have in accepting his general approach and yet hesitate to accept that it must also apply to the concept of Eternal Life.

For Phillips, beliefs about immortality, eternal life, the resurrection, if they are genuine, are *expressions of the state of*

---

98   *L.C.*, p. 56.
99   See I. Dilman's essay, 'Wittgenstein on the Soul' in the Royal Institute of Philosophy Lectures Vol. 7 1972–3 *Understanding Wittgenstein*, p. 189.
100 See *Death and Immortality* (Macmillan, 1970) and 'Angau a Thragwyddoldeb' (1967) in *Saith Ysgrif ar Grefydd*, pp. 119–38.
101 *The Tragic Sense of Life* (Fontana Library, 1962), p. 62.
102 'Y Syniad o Fywyd Tragwyddol' (The Idea of Eternal Life), *Y Dysgedydd*, Jan.–Feb. 1961, p. 20.

the soul.[103] He suggests that when Jesus said to the repentant thief, 'Today you will be with me in paradise', he was not foretelling the future. Rather, Jesus tells the thief that *because of the state of his soul*, he is part of the eternal; he shares God's Spirit.[104] If someone asked Phillips himself whether he expected to see his loved ones beyond the grave, his answer would be 'No'.[105] But in giving this answer Phillips claims that he is not denying the eternal. He too feels Unamuno's protest, 'Let me live!', but this is an expression of weakness rather than love for the eternal.[106] At one point Phillips comments on the difficulties which face a philosopher who is also a religious believer. Once the philosophical spirit has been awakened, it is too late to dream of days of peace and quiet.[107] Phillips' *Death and Immortality* (1970) is one of the most recent examples of his own loss of philosophical innocence. I will glance at the argument of that book before proceeding further.

Phillips begins by examining the common objection that obeying God's commands is pointless without survival or resurrection of some kind. His reply is that there is precisely no point for people who make this objection: 'It is only when a man has become absorbed by the love of God that he ceases to ask such questions, not because he is sure of his profit, but because profit has nothing to do with the character of his love. The immortality of his soul has to do, not with its existence after death . . . , but with his participation in God's life, in his contemplation of divine love.'[108] The reason for choosing the Christian way cannot be outside the quality of the life in Christ, if the belief is to be considered genuine.

Phillips had suggested the nature of his own alternative

---

[103] *Saith Ysgrif ar Grefydd*, p. 127.
[104] Ibid., p. 126.
[105] Ibid., p. 138.
[106] Ibid., p. 137.
[107] Ibid., p. 123.
[108] D.I., p. 38.

to the common views of the 'after life' in *Faith and Philo-sophical Enquiry*: 'I am not thinking . . . of immortality con-strued as survival, but of the radically different account . . . which is connected with purification and dying to the world.'[109] In *Death and Immortality* he develops this early statement by discussing the immortality of the soul in what he calls its 'natural setting'. The natural setting of terms like 'losing one's soul', 'selling one's soul', etc., is that of the *kind of life* a person is living.[110] So understood, all attempts to determine what kind of a 'thing' a soul is evaporate. The state of the believer's soul has to do with his possession of or lack of spirituality, assessed in terms of his relationship to God.[111] When a person dies, what he is, i.e., the state of his soul, is fixed for ever. The will of the dead cannot be changed. In the believer's case, his 'eternal destiny' at death is determined by his relationship to God. The destiny of an individual after his death cannot be changed by any 'temporal' predicate; his will is fixed for ever. Nevertheless, prayers for the dead may change the status of the dead *in God*.[112] In one respect there is no difference between the believer and the unbeliever, i.e., neither of them will survive their deaths. In another respect there is a great difference: 'For the believer, his death, like his life, is to be in God. For him, this is the life eternal which death cannot touch; the immortality which finally places the soul beyond the reach of the snares and temptation of this mortal life.'[113]

It is clear from Phillips' analysis that he not only questions the *religious* worth of survival or resurrection after death, but that he combines this with the *philosophical* conviction that there are no happenings after death.[114] He began his analysis in *Death and Immortality* by arguing that the logical

[109] F.P.E., pp. 262–3.
[110] D.I., p. 45.
[111] D.I., p. 48.
[112] D.I., p. 57.
[113] D.I., p. 60.
[114] *Saith Ysgrif ar Grefydd*, p. 127.

objections to the survival of disembodied spirits, non-material bodies or bodies rising after death are justified. He quickly moves on, however, to what he regards as his major task; namely that of asking whether the latter notions are necessary presuppositions to any belief in immortality, and whether an alternative account is available. I suggested earlier that Phillips' insistence on preserving the absolute reality of God and absolute worth of faith is closely related to his conviction that analytical philosophers must recognize the expressive and non-factual character of religious beliefs. But the point to notice here is that if we *could* speak intelligibly of survival or resurrection in factual terms, this would have little to do with genuine religion in Phillips' view. The general implication of Phillips' position, in fact, is that what we now call religious beliefs and values would be severely modified or even destroyed if an 'after life' were a *fact* about the universe. We can see here how closely Phillips' position resembles the point made by the early Wittgenstein:

> Not only is there no guarantee of the temporal immortality of the human soul, that is to say of its eternal survival after death; but, in any case, this assumption completely fails to accomplish the purpose for which it has always been intended. Or is some riddle solved by my surviving for ever? Is not this eternal life itself as much of a riddle as our present life? The solution of the riddle of life in space and time lies *outside* space and time.[115]

For someone's death to be really his *death*, there must be no continuation of life in any sense, through revival, survival or resurrection. It is because death marks the absolute end of life, suggests Phillips, that we talk of the majesty of death. We do not talk about the majesty of sleep.[116] The fact that death is real, that the grave really is a grave, enables Christians to speak with religious integrity

[115] T., 6.4312.
[116] F.P.E., p. 267.

about 'dying daily'. The nature of the daily death is then the only reason for so acting. In Kierkegaard's terms, the true Christian does not suffer from the 'reward disease'.[117]

Let me close this section with a specific example of what we might call genuine belief and genuine unbelief. Since I have just been discussing the religious response to death, it will concern believing and unbelieving perspectives on death and the dead. To say that the dead are dead, in response to a believer's faith about Eternal Life, is to say something which is correct, but trivially correct. It is to say something of which both believer and unbeliever are fully aware; the dead are dead. Believing and unbelieving views on death go beyond this bare assertion. The examples I have in mind are the contrasting views of Simone Weil and Friedrich Nietzsche. Simone Weil talks in a religious way about the Void, extinction, etc. Christian love *endures* the Void. It does not resort to fantasy to fill in the void created by the death of a friend.[118] The believer spurns all notions of compensation as he anticipates the void of his own extinction:

> To love truth means to endure the void and, as a result, to accept death. Truth is on the side of death.

> We must leave on one side the beliefs which fill up voids and sweeten what is bitter. The belief in immortality. The belief in the utility of sin: *etiam peccata*. The belief in the providential ordering of events—in short the 'consolations' which are ordinarily sought in religion.[119]

There is a very different perspective on death in Nietzsche's *My Sister and I*.[120] He anticipates his own death: 'Not the world is being annihilated, but I am; nature rejects ideas, even the most noble, in favour of mere animal existence:

---

[117] See *Purity of Heart*, pp. 60–69.
[118] *Gravity and Grace*, p. 21.
[119] Ibid., pp. 11 and 13.
[120] (Bridgehead Books, New York, 1965); this book apparently contains some of Nietzsche's last thoughts from his asylum at Jena.

Life is its own goal, and all my thoughts are as chaff in the wind of cosmic destiny.'[121] Nietzsche too speaks of the Void. But for him there is no value in accepting it. To accept the Void in Simone Weil's judgement is "supernatural".'[122] Nietzsche thinks that it is better simply to persist:

> Deprived of my last veil of illusion—the power of ideas—I gaze with terror upon the Void, but still I cling to existence, for the fact of mere existence is all that is left in the shattered landscape of the intellect. All reasoning is a mode of self-deception, but I cannot reason myself into a state of euphoria and imagine that I can find happiness in the realm of death, sunk deep in Nirvana. Oh, to be alive, to vegetate stupidly, but still to be *alive* and feel the warmth of the sun![123]

Nietzsche and Simone Weil are not divided by matters of fact. There is no theoretical argument here. Two value systems meet head on. It is some such conflict that reveals the genuine conflict between believer and unbeliever in the Wittgensteinian scheme.

---

[121] Ibid., p. 43.
[122] *Gravity and Grace*, p. 10.
[123] *My Sister and I*, p. 43.

CHAPTER FOUR

Organizing the Conflict

IN THIS chapter I shall follow up some of the problems suggested by the discussion so far. To set one foot on the Wittgensteinian road, in a sense, involves also the promise to walk the whole way. It is not a view which lends itself easily to modification by piecemeal criticism. To some extent this is an over-statement, but several critics of the Wittgensteinian approach have assumed that its 'weaknesses' can be overcome by adopting an ontology,[1] a concept of analogy,[2] and so on. Such suggestions underestimate the radicality of the approach in question. W. D. Hudson is one philosopher who has recognized the far-reaching consequences of Wittgenstein's ideas. Three basic questions remain, according to Hudson, when these ideas are applied to religious belief: (i) Is religious belief about something objectively real? (ii) Is it out of date? (iii) Is it rational?[3] Nevertheless, Hudson's way of putting the problems needs modification. One of the obvious features of the whole issue under discussion is that there are no mutually agreed terms which make it easy to mediate between conflicting views. The choice of terms indicates how the problem is already understood by the various disputants. Hudson's three questions show how he sees the problems at stake, but his questions are themselves question-begging. The first begs the question about 'real'; the second, about 'truth'; and the third, about 'rationality'.

---

[1] S. R. Sutherland, 'Religion and Ethics' *The Human World*, Nov. 1971, No. 5, p. 52; P. J. Sherry, 'Learning how to be Religious' *Theology*, Feb. 1974, pp. 81–90.

[2] P. J. Sherry, *Truth and the 'Religious Language Game'*, unpublished dissertation, Cambridge Univ. Ph.D. 1971, chap. 8.

[3] See Hudson's *Ludwig Wittgenstein*, pp. 68–71 and his *A Philosophical Approach to Religion* (Macmillan, London, 1974) *in toto*.

Some of the questions which arise from the present study are (i) Are religious beliefs distinctive? (ii) Is there a single concept of reality? (iii) Are religious beliefs relativized by the Wittgensteinians? (iv) Are they, in fact, discussing religion or a 'reduced' version of it?

Are Religious Beliefs Distinctive?

As we have seen, the Wittgensteinians do not claim that religious beliefs are *special kinds* of factual belief. Neither do they argue that such beliefs form a metaphysical system, even of the kind which is not subject to positivist criticism. Rather, they appear to be claiming that where 'religious' beliefs embody concepts from other modes of discourse, they are subject to the standards obtaining in those respective distinctive uses of language. Phillips argues, for example, that if someone's way of talking and acting implied that the efficacy of prayer for him was *causal*, then that person would have to justify his beliefs about prayer in terms of what we know of cause-effect relations.[4] The believer cannot claim that the cause-effect relation is being used in a peculiar sense and therefore not subject to demands for external justification. I hope it is clear from what I have been saying that the Wittgensteinians do not argue that no overtly 'religious' claim needs a justification. Factual 'religious' assertions certainly need to be justified. The implication is, however, that they forfeit their status as *religious* beliefs in the process of claiming to be factual in character.

It should be evident from the study so far that for a position like Phillips' to remain plausible, even on its own terms, he has to show how religious beliefs are *distinctive*, i.e., that they are not *other* kinds of belief in disguise. I said in the Introduction that the Wittgensteinian's entire effort was directed against reductionism in religion. Let me elaborate briefly. Wittgenstein and Phillips set themselves

---

4 See *C.P.*, p. 11.

against any attempt to go behind the religious observances or underneath the religious symbol in order to discover a *real* and underlying *purpose*. Phillips in particular criticizes Durkheim, Freud, Marett and Tylor for assuming that rational discourse *must* take a particular form, namely, the positivistic form which *they* assumed as normative for all men.[5] The anthropologists assumed that 'primitive' men thought that their religious observances were causally linked to the natural world. Consequently, the religion of the primitives was judged to be the fruit of ignorance and fear. But it was the anthropologists who were making 'mistakes'.

Phillips questions the sense of asking for reasons and purposes behind religious observances. Such observances grow out of the phenomena which make up a people's life; birth, death, harvest, the changes of seasons, the phases of the moon, etc.[6] Primitive peoples certainly felt the impact of these things. Why ask for a *reason* for this? If a lament is sung after the death of a loved one, it is very foolish to ask for a reason for this.[7] The religious responses derive from the possibilities extant in the language and life of a people. No one can *prescribe* what particular language-games should develop around such phenomena or *judge* them in the light of other systems. This kind of argument constitutes a legitimate stand against attempts to provide a genetic or reductionist account of religion in general. However, problems emerge when one attempts to show the distinctive character of, for example, Judaeo-Christian beliefs. Phillips succeeds in distinguishing 'religious' beliefs and observances from reductionist explanations in purely functionalist terms of, say, the body's or society's psychological or biological needs, e.g., that people burn effigies or kiss photographs *in*

---

[5] See Phillips' essay 'Crefydd a Metaffiseg' (1971) ('Religion and Meta-physics') in *Athronyddu am Grefydd*, esp. pp. 27–31; see also pp. 84, 92–5 in the same book.

[6] Ibid., pp. 28–9.

[7] This example derives originally from R. Rhees—see *Athronyddu am Grefydd*, p. 29.

order to gain satisfaction.[8] What is open to question, how-ever, is whether Phillips establishes that religious beliefs—and primarily those of the Judaeo-Christian tradition—are distinctive in the sense that they can be distinguished from many kinds of human responses to natural and social phenomena.

When faced with the charge that he is really treating religious beliefs as simply 'attitudes to life', Phillips replies as follows:

> . . . In some contexts this way of talking is unobjectionable, but it can be misleading. It may suggest that religious responses to the world are in the same logical category as 'bearing things with equanimity', 'making the best of a bad situation', 'taking a long-term view of things', etc. What such a categorization neglects is the way in which the worship of God makes the believer's relationship to other people and the events which befall him substantially different; that is to say, without his belief he could not be said to have the same relationship or experience the same events. The believer's worship must make the world a wholly different one.[9]

In one sense Phillips is obviously right in claiming that religious beliefs do not belong to the same logical category as human attitudes so tepidly expressed in the examples he gives. Nevertheless, the question I wish to raise is whether Phillips shows that the more radical expressions of depend-ence on how things go, the contemplation of *that* we are and *that* the world is, etc., belong to a logical category which is peculiarly religious. In the above passage Phillips argues that the idea of worship, whatever else we say, puts religious belief into a category of its own. I shall argue that this might be true when said of many other ways of conceiving religious belief, but is much less obvious in the light of Phillips' general position.

A factor which we must always have in mind when

8 See my earlier comments on Wittgenstein's notes on Frazer.
9 *F.P.E.*, p. 55.

discussing the Wittgensteinian view is that 'God' is in no sense a substantive. Thus, when Phillips speaks of God as, say, 'giving' something,[10] we must not think that this refers in any literal or metaphysical sense to an agent performing an act. This is a *way of speaking* in religion which is unobjectionable provided that we do not import any notion of reference. God can certainly be found in the language religious people have learned to use; that is, we discover the *sense* of speaking of God in the language they use. But they are not referring to anything outside of themselves, except in the sense that we speak of values which are not *in* the world. Phillips would add to this, of course, that one must take account of how God is understood in the context of worship. Let me pursue the question at issue in this section by taking a specific example.

Albert Camus provides a brief but vivid account of a picture which could arguably form the framework for an atheist-humanist's life, namely, *The Myth of Sisyphus*.[11] Camus draws the picture of his 'absurd hero', Sisyphus, the 'proletarian of the gods', who is fated endlessly to push a huge stone up a steep slope: 'Then Sisyphus watches the stone rush down in a few moments toward that lower world whence he will have to push it up again toward the summit. He goes back down to the plain.'[12] It is the use which Sisyphus makes of his breathing space that lifts him above his circumstances and turns the story into a tragedy:

> It is during that return, that pause, that Sisyphus interests me . . . At each of those moments when he leaves the heights and gradually sinks toward the lairs of the gods, he is superior to his fate. He is stronger than his rock.
> . . . Sisyphus . . . knows the whole extent of his wretched condition: it is what he thinks of during his descent. The lucidity that was to constitute his torture at the same time

[10] E.g., *C.P.*, pp. 74f.
[11] Vintage Books, (New York, 1955), pp. 88–91.
[12] Ibid., p. 89.

crowns his victory. There is no fate that cannot be surmounted by scorn.[13]

Camus links Sisyphus' condition with the cry of Oedipus: 'Despite so many ordeals, my advanced age and the nobility of my soul make me conclude that all is well.'[14] In such a cry we see the secret of Sisyphus' silent joy. For Camus, that cry is sacred: 'It makes of fate a human matter, which must be settled among men.'[15] Camus concludes with Sisyphus' acceptance that the rock will be there again at his descent: 'But Sisyphus teaches the higher fidelity that negates the gods and raises rocks. He too concludes that all is well . . . The struggle itself toward the heights is enough to fill a man's heart. One must imagine Sisyphus happy.'[16]

The Myth of Sisyphus is a very powerful expression of one way of responding to the apparent indifference of the universe towards man. This expression is also weakly conceived if we describe it as an attitude of 'making the best of a bad situation', etc. Like Phillips' 'eternal' view, it acknowledges its total dependence on the way things go. Sisyphus' view, like the faith of Phillips' believer, is, in a sense, not *of* the world; his scorn surmounts anything which his fate offers. Sisyphus does not despair; he too can say that all is well.

It would not be difficult to imagine someone responding to the human condition in the way displayed by Camus' mythological Sisyphus. Indeed, Camus himself may have conceived part or most of his own life in such a framework. Camus is famous for believing that life is absurd. Yet he saw the need to affirm values in the midst of absurdity. 'I chose justice,' says Camus, 'in order to remain faithful to the Earth.'[17] In his essay, 'The Enigma', Camus says the follow-

13 Ibid., pp. 89–90.
14 Ibid., p. 90.
15 Ibid., p. 91.
16 Ibid., p. 91.
17 Quoted by J. Onimus, *Albert Camus and Christianity* (Gill & Macmillan, Dublin, 1970), p. 77.

ing: 'In our darkest nihilism I have sought only reasons to go beyond it . . . by an instinctive fidelity to a light in which I was born, and in which for thousands of years men have learned to welcome life even in suffering.'[18] In his brief essay, 'Return to Tipasa', Camus also uses the metaphor of 'light' to refer to an unquenchable renewal that occurs when some men are brought face to face with their inexorable fate, the given, 'that strength which . . . helps me to accept what exists once I have recognized that I cannot change it.'[19] At one point in the essay Camus' personal position seems close to the Sisyphus myth. Camus had seen again the ruins of Tipasa with which he associated an earlier vision, an earlier lucidity:

> . . . I had always known that the ruins of Tipasa were younger than our new buildings or our crumbling towns. There, the world was born again each morning in a light that was always new. O light! This is the cry of all the characters who, in classical tragedy, come face to face with their destiny. Their final refuge was also ours, and I now knew that this was so. In the depths of the winter I finally learned that there lay in me an unconquerable summer.[20]

The point of this digression into the spirituality of Camus is to show that Phillips' account of the distinctive characteristics of religious beliefs can be closely paralleled by the 'eternal' view of a man who vigorously held that Christianity was an illusion.[21] Phillips, particularly in *The Concept of Prayer*,[22] argues that religious beliefs are concerned with *that* things are. The believer's radical acceptance of the 'given' comes out very strongly in that study. The believer gives up all claims and expectations about what the world owes to him, and, therefore, prayer is not in any sense an

---

18 Albert Camus, *Selected Essays and Notebooks* (Penguin Books, 1970), p. 145.
19 Ibid., p. 148.
20 Ibid., p. 152.
21 See *Albert Camus and Christianity*, p. 36.
22 C.P., pp. 63–80.

attempt to manipulate what may happen. Camus' Sisyphus symbolizes a secular response to contingency which is very similar to Phillips' believer. Of course, the traditions which inform Camus' and Phillips' responses are very different. Camus' 'divinity' lurks on the beaches of Algiers and is connected with the light his native land had known for thousands of years in the midst of their sufferings. Phillips' 'divinity' hails from Palestine and is related to the sufferings of the Jews and particularly to one Jew, Jesus of Nazareth. Thus the vocabulary and concepts which both Camus and Phillips use to *express* their commitment will clearly be different. Yet is this a reason for putting their positions into logically different categories in the strong sense that Phillips' general position seems to demand?

I noted earlier how Phillips stressed the substantial difference which worship makes to the believer.[23] The question is what force is to be ascribed to 'substantially different' here. When Phillips speaks of God 'giving' something to the believer, he does not have any kind of heavenly agent in mind. There is no 'giver' in that sense. The believer 'receives' the gift through *contemplation*.[24] It is, of course, perfectly in order for Phillips to argue that this does not mean that religious beliefs are totally subjective. The believer did not invent the religious tradition itself. Indeed, he does contemplate something other than himself,[25] in the sense that he is so reliant on the tradition, and that the religious view of people and things is not 'from the midst of them'. Yet Camus also contemplates something other than himself. He too is reliant upon his predecessors' defiance of suffering, and his view involves a radical acceptance *that* rather than *how* the world is.

When we take Phillips' advice and look to see what is real for the believer by paying attention to the language he

23 See *F.P.E.*, p. 55.
24 *C.P.*, p. 75.
25 *C.P.*, p. 68.

uses and the roles the beliefs play in his life, we are bound to see the similarities between Phillips' believer and the atheist Camus. Phillips uses terms like 'God', 'grace', 'sacrifice', etc., and Camus uses 'unconquerable summer', 'fate', 'the given', etc., to express what is substantially the same approach to life. The *difference* is in the language they use. The term 'God' has a very wide religious usage and the phrase 'unconquerable summer' is presumably private to Camus. Nevertheless, they both perform the same expressive function. They will obviously *mean* different things. Yet to put them alongside each other helps us to see how much they have in common as expressive responses to the contingency of the world. Phillips' believer and Camus may *contemplate* in different ways, but their understanding of the human condition is basically the same. Camus' Sisyphus and Phillips' Job are co-partners in the same struggle.

To summarize, for someone who wishes to maintain a substantive reference for God, Phillips will hardly satisfy what they understand by the distinctive character of religious belief. From that point of view, the words of Sisyphus apply to Phillips as well as Camus—fate is a 'human matter' which is settled among men.[26] Phillips' 'religion' would only be distinctive as a quixotic brand of atheism. Putting aside for the moment this kind of reaction to Phillips, we could say that he does distinguish non-referential theism from 'non-referential' atheism.[27] The difference is in the language and in what it means. This will not be a sufficient difference for many people. Religious belief, for them, will have been reduced and relativized. I shall return to these charges later, but first I shall discuss the question of a single concept of reality.

---

[26] *The Myth of Sisyphus*, p. 91.
[27] 'Referential' atheism would be the type which based itself on a denial that there exists a being called 'God' who is 'there' in a similar way that the planets are there. 'Non-referential' atheism simply has no place or use for the language of religion. (cf. *C.P.*, p. 19.)

A Single Concept of Reality?

At one point[28] Phillips refers to the way in which a mistaken epistemology is used to reject religious belief. The mistake is to assume that there is a standard use of ordinary language which provides a norm for all uses. When judged against this norm, religious language is classed as either meaningless or meaningful but false. Phillips goes on to say that Winch's essay, 'Understanding a Primitive Society'[29] is helpful as a start towards questioning this philosophical rejection of religion. For Phillips and Winch the idea of a single concept of reality is an abstraction which exists only in the minds of philosophers. Winch describes his own essay as critical of 'some forms of the idea that there is, or can be, a conception of "a world" to be understood, which conception is independent of forms of social life and can provide us with criteria by reference to which we can criticize as "irrational" certain ways in which men do live.'[30] This abstracted idea of 'a world' can be made up of several lesser abstractions. For example, in a recent essay,[31] Phillips argues that an abstracted concept of reasonableness is latent in much contemporary moral philosophy. He sketches the six characteristics of the 'reasonable man' presupposed by those writings. But this 'familiar friend' does not exist.[32]

The 'concept of factuality' is another abstraction in the minds of philosophers.[33] Winch argues against Popper's idea that there is a basic difference between the norms of behaviour (logically akin to decisions), conventional in a society, and the laws of nature which are established and

---

[28] R.U., p. 4; see also F.P.E., p. 17.
[29] *Ethics and Action*, pp. 8–49. For a sympathetic criticism of this important essay see H. O. Mounce's 'Understanding a Primitive Society' *Philosophy*, Oct. 1973 Vol. 48.
[30] *Ethics and Action*, p. 2.
[31] 'Allegiance and Change in Morality: A Study in Contrasts', *Philosophy and the Arts* (Macmillan, London, 1973), pp. 47–64.
[32] Ibid., p. 49.
[33] Winch discusses this in 'Nature and Convention', *Ethics and Action*, pp. 50–72.

presupposed in all the sciences. According to Winch, the view suggested by Popper's discussion is ' "Facts are *there*, whereas decisions have to be *made*".'[34] Popper ignores the way in which the formulation of laws of nature also emerge from particular societies. Winch argues:

> . . . we cannot say without qualification that modern scientific theories are about the same set of facts as the theories of earlier stages of scientific development were about . . . scientific *concepts* have changed . . ., and with them scientists' views on what is to count as a relevant fact . . . this does not mean that earlier scientists had a *wrong* idea of what the facts were; they had the idea appropriate to the investigations *they* were conducting.[35]

Winch continues: 'We may be able to say that particular facts are given, but that is not to say that the concept of factuality is given; it arises out of the way men live.'[36] This suggests just how complex the issue becomes when this view is applied to religious traditions which persist over centuries. Concepts of reality, rationality, etc., may not only differ horizontally across the contemporary forms of life, but they differ vertically down through the ages of man. There is no space to relate this problem fully to the current debate about 'paradigms' in the philosophy of science, but we can grasp what is involved here by a striking example from T. S. Kuhn:

> Consider . . . the men who called Copernicus mad because he proclaimed that the earth moved. They were not either just wrong or quite wrong. Part of what they meant by 'earth' was fixed position. Their earth, at least, could not be moved. Correspondingly, Copernicus' innovation was not simply to move the earth. Rather, it was a whole new way of regarding the problems of physics and astronomy, one that necessarily changed the meaning of both 'earth' and 'motion'.[37]

[34] Ibid., p. 56.
[35] Ibid., p. 53.
[36] Ibid., pp. 56–7.
[37] *The Structure of Scientific Revolutions* (Univ. of Chicago Press, 1973 ed.),

Once we see the force of Winch's and Kuhn's points, the problems of assuming a concept of factuality native to Hebrew culture, two thousand or more years ago, become immense. Winch's case is well argued and clearly there cannot be a simple notion 'the facts' which is not itself 'theory-laden'. But what Winch says of the concept of factuality would apply also to notions of 'exist' and 'real', i.e., that they are *context-dependent* notions. Winch's point reminds us of a familiar distinction drawn by philosophers. W. D. Hudson, for example, draws a distinction between the two 'general meanings' attributed to 'real' and 'exist'.[38] T. R. Miles draws a similar distinction and uses the terms (i) 'contextual existence' and (ii) 'metaphysical existence'.[39] When 'exist' or 'real' are used in the first sense (contextual existence) their meaning depends upon the context. The question, 'Do dodos still exist?' and 'have I really a duty to relieve human suffering?' are intelligible within the context of material object discourse and the moral universe of discourse respectively.

To ask (ii) 'Does the physical world exist?' or 'Does moral obligation really exist?' is to ask questions of a different kind from (i) (above). The questions under (i) can be answered in principle because they presuppose that the decision to think scientifically or morally has already been made; experience has been framed in a particular way. But what of the criteria for answering the second kind of question? One would need a single overall field of discourse within which such questions could be located and answered by reference to the constitutive concepts of that field. If such an all-embracing

---

pp. 149–50. See also I. Lakatos & A. Musgrave, eds. *Criticism and the Growth of Knowledge* (C.U.P., 1970); J. Ziman, *Public Knolwedge* (C.U.P., 1968); R. Trigg, *Reason and Commitment* (C.U.P., 1973). For an assessment of the significance of this development for religious belief, see B. Mitchell, *The Justification of Religious Belief* (Macmillan, 1973), pp. 64–70; 76–84, and I. G. Barbour, *Myths, Models and Paradigms* (S.C.M., 1974).

[38] 'On Two Points Against Wittgensteinian Fideism', *Philosophy* (1968) 43, pp. 269–73, esp. p. 272.

[39] *Religion and the Scientific Outlook* (Allen & Unwin, London, 1959), p. 43.

field of discourse could be found, it would still, of course, make sense to ask whether something which was in accord with these criteria is real.

This is a difficult area for discussion and it may be a help to clear up a possible point of confusion about the Wittgensteinian stake in this wide-ranging debate about rationality, paradigms, etc. In so far as they make points about religious belief, Phillips and Winch are not claiming that religious beliefs could be hypotheses, enclosed within the religious mode of discourse and enjoying immunity from the demands for confirmation and justification normally met in the real world. They do not stress the *diversity* of the criteria of rationality for *that* reason. Winch does show, of course, how careful we must be in handling the concept of factuality —how earlier scientists may have had different concepts, etc.—but this should not mislead us into thinking that he is attempting to *ease* the standards of verification, etc., where factual claims are made in certain areas, for example, primitive societies. Phillips and Winch stress the diversity of criteria to overcome what Wittgenstein called a 'craving for generality' which seduces us into misunderstanding certain practices and beliefs and which is instrumental in giving some uses of language a culturally privileged status. A critical essay by Meynell[40] illustrates the strength of the hold such a 'craving' may have. Arguing against both Winch and Phillips and using his own terminology, Meynell asserts that while 'subjective worlds' may be different from one another (e.g., the 'subjective world' of the theist is different from the 'subjective world' of the atheist), the 'objective world' is the same for everybody. Meynell means that while, for example, electrons did not exist in the 'subjective worlds' of scientists before they were discovered, they have always existed in the 'objective world'. Granted this crude distinction, Meynell then attempts to show that there is a 'critical

---

[40] H. Meynell, 'Truth, Witchcraft and Professor Winch' *The Heythrop Journal*, May 1972, pp. 162–72.

attitude' either explicit or implicit, in varying degrees, wherever language is used:

> . . . every subjective world consists of a mesh of assumptions about what is the case; and that subjective worlds approximate to the objective world so far as these assumptions would, if they were put to the test, turn out to be justified. Every subjective world is, in fact, a complex of more or less explicit hypotheses about the objective world, *whatever other function it may have in regulating the lives and feelings of those who share it*; and the critical attitude consists in making these assumptions explicit, testing them, and rejecting those that turn out to be false.[41]

It is the sentence in italics here which illustrates the mistaken epistemology Winch and Phillips are anxious to deny. A craving for generality has encouraged Meynell to assert that *every* so-called 'subjective world' is 'a complex of more or less explicit hypotheses about the objective world'. One is bound to ask what this kind of approach would in fact make of a 'subjective world' dominated by an expressive, non-referential use of language? The odds are that it would not understand it as such, and would make it out to be something it is not. The main issue at stake between the Wittgensteinians and the kind of view represented by Meynell is whether genuine religious belief is of such an expressive, non-referential kind, or whether it makes 'more or less explicit' claims about what is the case. One of the most vigorous opponents of the Wittgensteinian approach, Kai Nielsen, has argued in a similar way to Meynell. Nielsen thinks that the various forms of language, e.g., moral, religious and legal discourse, etc., are part of the same overall 'conceptual structure'. He has suggested some *non-contextual* criteria:

> . . . 'rational' and 'reasonable' . . . are not so contextual that in any form of life a man could properly be said to have a 'rational

---

[41] Ibid., p. 165. My italics.

belief' if it were not an impartial belief and if, when a question was raised about the belief, he was not prepared, where it was practicable, to weigh the evidence or reasons pro and con for the claim in question before making a decision to act in a certain way or to continue to hold a certain belief.[42]

This is a craving for generality with a vengeance. If this concept is applied as univerally as Nielsen suggests it should be, religious beliefs—of the 'absolute' kind which the Wittgensteinians stress—appear to be irrational. As we have seen, if religious 'pictures' do constitute the all-regulating frameworks for a person's life, one can hardly have an 'extra' reason for adopting them. The use of an overall conceptual structure then puts these kinds of religious beliefs under pressure. They are made to look irrational or simply untrue. Where the religious believer himself accepts the all-embracing concept of reality, the sense of God's absolute reality is threatened. If two people disagree about the earth's distance from the sun, their respective claims have a *relative* reality in the sense that they are related to the standards of enquiry which obtain in astronomy. The standard itself is an absolute one. In the case of the reality of God, Phillips is anxious to show that this reality is not subject to a broader common measure. The reality of God is absolute; it is *itself* a common measure for judging what it makes sense to say in the religious forms of life.

An alternative to Nielsen's way of talking would be to ask whether there is a *common core* to all uses of 'fact', 'existence' and 'reality', whilst respecting different uses in different contexts. John Hick has asked this kind of question and suggests that the idea of 'making a difference' is the notion common to 'fact', 'existence', etc.:

To say that x exists or is real, that it is a fact that there is an x, is to claim that the character of the universe differs in some specific way from the character that an x-less universe would

42 'Wittgensteinian Fideism Again: A Reply to Hudson' *Philosophy*, 1969, 44, p. 64.

have. The nature of this difference will naturally depend upon the character of the x in question.[43]

This appears to be more tolerant than Nielsen's way of putting the matter. It allows, in principle, for a believer to make out a case for 'religious facts' rather than insisting that his claims are *either* straightforwardly factual *or* irrational. The possibility of this more tolerant way has encouraged philosophers like the late Ian T. Ramsey and Hick himself to formulate positions in which 'it is *a sort of fact* that God exists'.[44] Nevertheless, there is in this alternative way itself an *either/or* which would never satisfy the Wittgensteinians. This is that if religious beliefs do not make claims about an 'objective reference', they are *merely* subjective attitudes to the world.[45]

If Phillips and Winch can show that there are uses of language, expressive, non-referential uses whose meanings are lost if put in any other way, then much of what they criticize about the idea of an all-embracing concept of reality is valid. However, in making out his case, Phillips seems to have over-reacted in a way which sometimes distorts his own case. A remark of Flew's in his review of Phillips' *Death and Immortality* illustrates the point. Flew refers to Chapter Three of Phillips' book which contains the latter's attempt to develop a doctrine of immortality. Flew comments, 'Thus he points out, *curiously as if expecting opposition from the present reviewer*, that there are colloquial expressions containing the word *soul* in which this certainly does not have to be interpreted as a word for a substance.'[46] In the context of the present discussion, Flew's protest amounts to a retort that he is not using an all-embracing concept of reality. He does

---

[43]   *Philosophy of Religion* (Prentice-Hall, New Jersey, 1973), p. 96.

[44]   I. T. Ramsey, *Christian Empiricism* (ed. J. H. Gill) (Sheldon Press, London, 1974), p. 239.

[45]   See I. T. Ramsey, *Models for Divine Activity* (S.C.M., London, 1973), p. 57; J. Hick, *God and the Universe of Faiths* (Macmillan, London, 1973), pp. 23–4.

[46]   *Philosophical Books* May 1971, Vol. XII No. 2, p. 23. (My italics).

not assume that the word 'soul' as used in 'He'd sell his soul for money' entails a philosophical theory about the duality of human nature. It might be worth saying here just what is the disagreement between Phillips and Flew. As we have seen, Flew is not saying that 'soul' must come to the same thing in every context of language. Phillips agrees with Flew that there are no events after death, and Flew refers to this in his review:

> Perhaps . . . it is of more than merely autobiographical interest to say to Phillips that when about twenty years ago I first began in the Socratic Club at Oxford and elsewhere to air the conclusions which we now share these were attacked as far-fetched, as factitious, as disingenuous, and of course as false; but never as irrelevant to the Christian hope of resurrection and immortality.[47]

Flew raises a question here which I have mentioned from time to time in this book. That is, just what kind of belief is it to which notions of factual reference, etc., are irrelevant? If that kind of belief is also genuine religion, the consequences are very far-reaching. It is not only old members of the Socratic Club who have mistaken the grammar of belief but the majority of contemporary philosophers of religion. Before asking more closely whether it is true religion, or 'religion' at all, I will discuss the question of relativism which I mentioned in the previous section.

The Question of Relativism

Gellner has tersely put an objection often levelled against the Wittgensteinian view: 'For most modern thinkers, relativism is a *problem*: for Winch and Wittgenstein, it is a *solution* . . . Wittgenstein and Winch *arrive* at relativism, they don't start out from it.'[48] Gellner thinks that Wittgenstein's relativism is given as a solution to the problem of meaning.

---

[47]   Ibid., p. 24.
[48]   *Cause and Meaning in the Social Sciences*, p. 67.

That is meaning is not the mirroring of the thing meant, it is the possession of a role and a place in a 'language' or a 'form of life'. Gellner believes that Wittgenstein was too exhausted in the end to realize the enormous problems that arise once he had arrived at this position.[49] According to other critics, the particular brand of relativism that Wittgenstein and Phillips are alleged to fall victim to is that of 'conceptual relativism'.[50] Let us attempt to clear the ground and locate the precise problem facing Wittgenstein and Phillips.

For several years now some of the issues have been fully discussed by the social scientists in general and by the anthropologists in particular.[51] Wittgenstein and Phillips are directly connected with this wider debate. Winch used Wittgenstein's ideas in his writings on ethics and the social sciences,[52] and Phillips used Winch's work as a model for the philosophy of religion. The anthropologist's attempt to understand a primitive society resembles the philosopher's attempt to understand religious belief.[53] Winch believes that cross-cultural understanding is possible, but he is critical of certain ways of attempting this.[54] Similarly, Phillips thinks that philosophers can understand religious belief with due regard to the difficulties involved.[55] Some of the problems disappear when we realize that Winch and Phillips are *not* advocating the impossibility of non-participants understanding either primitive societies or religious beliefs.

What then is the threat of relativism? Nielsen argues that with 'just a little twist',[56] 'Wittgensteinian fideism' can favour a profound form of scepticism: 'To be such a con-

---

49 Ibid., pp. 67f.
50 See K. Nielsen, *Contemporary Critiques of Religion* (Macmillan, London, 1971), pp. 94–111, and R. Trigg, *Reason and Commitment*.
51 See all of the essays in B. Wilson (ed.) *Rationality* (Blackwell, Oxford, 1970), and J. Ladd (ed.) *Ethical Relativism* (Wadsworth, California, 1973).
52 See Winch's *Ethics and Action* and *The Idea of a Social Science*.
53 See R.U., p. 4.
54 *Ethics and Action*, pp. 3, 38.
55 C.P., p. 83.
56 *Contemporary Critiques of Religion*, p. 98.

ceptual relativist is to argue that what is to count as knowledge, evidence, truth, a fact, an observation, making sense
and the like is uniquely determined by the linguistic framework used. But since our very conceptions of intelligibility,
validity, knowledge and the like are a function of the
linguistic system we use, it is impossible for us to attain a
neutral Archimedean point in virtue of which we could
evaluate the comparative adequacy of our own and other
linguistic frameworks.'[57] For Nielsen, whatever the consequences conceptual relativism may have for any particular
realm of discourse, they *must* prove disastrous for religious
belief. This must follow, according to Nielsen, because
religious beliefs make assumptions about the nature of
reality or ultimate reality.[58]

Any discussion of the charge of relativism in the present
context must consider a key passage from Winch which
provides a way in to see Phillips' essential position:

> Reality is not what gives language sense. What is real and
> what is unreal shows itself *in* the sense that language has . . .
> We can imagine a language with no concept of, say, wetness,
> but hardly one in which there is no way of distinguishing the
> real from the unreal. Nevertheless we could not in fact distin-
> guish the real from the unreal without understanding the way
> this distinction operates in the language.[59]

For Wittgenstein and Phillips the forms of language are
inseparably bound to the forms of life. But the forms of life
are as varied as their corresponding conceptions of truth,
rationality and intelligibility. It must follow, therefore, that
it is irrational to claim to say what reality is like in itself
quite apart from the assumptions of the distinctive norms of
rationality, intelligibility and reality in specific language-
games. It is at this point that it is tempting to say that if the
latter are *all* 'right' or 'true', how can any meaning still be

[57] Ibid., p. 96.
[58] Ibid., pp. 105-6.
[59] Quoted in *C.P.*, p. 9.

attached to those words? Nevertheless, it is a mistake to frame the question in that way.

Phillips himself is anxious to avoid what he calls 'Protagorean relativism': '. . . it must make a difference whether we say one thing rather than another; there must be a distinction between what is rational and what is irrational. To abandon such a distinction would . . . plunge us "straight into an extreme Protagorean relativism." '[60] His most detailed treatment of the threat of relativism to his views is in the context of his discussions of moral practices.[61] Phillips and Mounce distinguish their own view from the relativism of Protagoras. They believe that there are two possible interpretations of Protagoras' statement that man is the measure of all things, namely, (i) the opinions of any individual are necessarily correct, or (ii) the opinions held by the majority are correct. Phillips' view *differs* from (i) because, for him, an individual's judgements on morality derive their sense from the practices of the moral community to which he belongs; the individual is not himself the measure of right and wrong. Phillips' position *resembles* (ii) in so far as Protagoras was right in saying that human agreement is a necessary condition for there to be concepts of truth and falsity.[62] The point of difference is that, for Protagoras, the agreement of the majority is not merely the necessary condition for the ideas of truth and falsity; it is *itself the measure* of the latter.[63] By contrast, for Phillips—following Wittgenstein—the *measure* is the *generally applied criterion* found in an ongoing form of life. In Wittgenstein's words: 'It is what human beings *say* that is true and false; and they agree in the *language* they use. That is not agreement in opinions but in form of life.'[64]

[60] C.P., pp. 8–9.
[61] With H. O. Mounce in *Moral Practices*, pp. 61–78; see also *Athronyddu am Grefydd*, pp. 25, 32.
[62] M.P., p. 62.
[63] M.P., p. 63.
[64] P.I., 241.

Agreement formed simply by the opinions of the majority is *convention* in the narrow sense of the term. Phillips' view is agreement in the wider and deeper sense of convention implied in Wittgenstein's idea of a form of life. On Phillips' view, it is not absurd for the minority to be applying the conventionally agreed criteria correctly and the majority to be mistaken.[65] Individuals do not form their views in logical privacy and subsequently come to some mutual agreement with the majority. Rather it is the commitment to the form of social life which makes it intelligible to hold particular opinions.

What then can we make of the charge of relativism? Both Wittgenstein and Phillips rule out the idea of an 'objective reality' against which all commitments may be measured. However, it is a mistake to frame an objection in the following way: '. . . if, from within a particular system or form of life, we say that, therefore, all systems are "right", then this term is emptied of any useful meaning; if we claim superiority for our own linguistic framework we are simply being ethno- or lingua-centric.' This appears to be the way Nielsen sees the problem,[66] and it distorts the true position of Phillips and Wittgenstein. A glance at some remarks Wittgenstein made to Rush Rhees in 1945 should bring this out:

> Someone may say, 'There is still the difference between truth and falsity. Any ethical judgement in whatever system may be true or false.' Remember that 'P is true' means simply 'P'. If I say: 'Although I believe that so and so is good, I may be wrong': this says no more than that what I assert may be denied.
>
> Or suppose someone says, 'One of the ethical systems must be the right one—or nearer to the right one.' Well, suppose I say Christian ethics is the right one. Then I am making a judgement of value. It amounts to *adopting* Christian ethics. It is not

[65] *M.P.*, p. 64.
[66] *Contemporary Critiques of Religion*, p. 96.

like saying that one of these physical theories must be the right one. The way in which some reality corresponds—or conflicts—with a physical theory has no counterpart here.

If you say there are various systems of ethics you are not saying they are all equally right. That means nothing. Just as it would have no meaning to say that each was right from his own standpoint. That could only mean that each judges as he does.[67]

These short passages make explicit much which is implied in both Wittgenstein and Phillips. They refer here to ethical systems but there is little doubt that Wittgenstein would have applied his view in the same way to religious beliefs.

Wittgenstein rejects the idea of any analogy between claiming that an ethical theory is true and claiming that 'some reality corresponds—or conflicts—with a physical theory.' Therefore, it is inappropriate to speak of (i) a particular ethical system as being 'right' in the sense of its competing with other *theories* in representing what is in fact the case; (ii) of all ethical systems being equally right ('that means nothing'); and (iii) an ethical system as *right for him* ('right from his own standpoint. That could only mean that each judges as he does.'). For Wittgenstein, to speak of the 'rightness' or 'wrongness' of commitments is simply to talk of the commitments actually *adopted*.

This standpoint is consistent with his view that ethical systems (and religious beliefs) are not hypotheses or beliefs which have a propositional element. They are expressions of value. If they were hypotheses, it would make sense to speak of ethical systems as being 'right', or right for *him*, and so on. Therefore, it is inappropriate for Nielsen to criticize Phillips and Wittgenstein as 'conceptual relativists'. This charge would only be apposite if those philosophers regarded religious beliefs as propositional theories. In another context, Wittgenstein uses the term 'world-picture' for a basic, non-

[67] R. Rhees, *Discussions of Wittgenstein* (Routledge and Kegan Paul, London, 1970), p. 101.

hypothetical commitment.[68] The basic commitment determines what is to count as a reason, and so reasons cannot be given for the commitment or world-picture.

This brief discussion should have shown that to call the Wittgensteinians 'conceptual relativists' is a mistake granted the views those philosophers actually hold. However, could we not say that this clarification has changed the threat from that of relativism to that of *arbitrariness*. Is it simply a happy sociological and psychological coincidence that believers *adopt* the beliefs they do? This question is closely related to the issue of whether it is an arbitrary matter that we have the moral rules to which we adhere. Phillips (with Mounce) argues that we do not regard our moral practices as something we justify by appealing to wider considerations: 'Telling the truth rather than lying, respecting life rather than killing, being generous rather than mean, etc., are things which we take to be right as a matter of course.'[69] Some philosophers, however, ask *why* we have these practices and *why* we adhere to them. A variety of answers have been offered; *because* they satisfy the needs of society, lead to social cohesion, or promote the greatest good and happiness of the greatest number, etc. Phillips rejects all such attempts to give non-moral foundations to morality. But he also thinks that the mistake of attempting to justify moral practices as such ignores the moral implications involved in the very notion of social existence.[70]

Does any of this have implications for the treatment of the question of *why* people have the religious commitments they have? For example, is it possible to pick up Phillips' comment that the very notion of society has moral implications and say that the very notion of human existence has religious implications? W. D. Hudson seems to have this in mind in the following:

[68] *O.C.*, 167.
[69] *M.P.*, p. 20.
[70] *M.P.*, pp. 20–21.

Some language-games, or forms of life, seem to be definitive of humanity in the sense that it is essential to our concept of man, as man, that he should engage in them. Morality would be a case in point. It is, I suppose, conceivable that men should cease to use moral language: that words such as 'right', 'good', 'ought', as they are now used in a moral sense, should drop out of our language . . . I say that this is conceivable; but when we imagine it, do we not have to add that, if it happened to *homo sapiens*, he would be deprived of something essential to what we have always meant by his humanity—in a real sense, he would cease to be a man?

What I suggest, very tentatively, is that somewhat the same might be said of religious belief.[71]

Whatever the merits of Hudson's suggestion, it is extremely doubtful whether such a development of the Wittgensteinian view I have been discussing is possible. Phillips' Introduction to J. L. Stocks' *Morality and Purpose* is relevant here. Phillips refers to the view that what are regarded as virtues are connected with the *needs* of man. This view hopes for a positive theory of human nature: 'Just as a plant needs certain things in order to flourish, might it not be the case that man needs certain things in order to flourish too? The actions which would satisfy those needs would be actions which men *ought* to perform.'[72] This approach would therefore create an ideal marriage between morality and rationality: 'The positive theory of human nature is thought of as essentially descriptive, and to say that something ought to be done would be to state an obvious fact.'[73] Thus, if this view were applied to religious belief, the ambiguous frontier between facts and values would be broken down. The religious beliefs would not be upheld by our confidence in them, however unshakeable, but by their grounding in the very idea of *homo sapiens*. It is difficult to see how one could give such an account of human nature without smuggling

[71] *Ludwig Wittgenstein*, p. 71.
[72] *Morality and Purpose*, pp. 5–6.
[73] Ibid., p. 6.

in an evaluative presupposition about what a 'man' is. The circularity involved is similar to that found in Bonhoeffer's statement, that to be a Christian is what it really means to be a man.[74] It begs the question about what it is to be human.

The question that arises, however, is not whether this particular attempt to answer the threat of arbitrariness is adequate or not, but whether *any* answer could be. Once one attempts to go behind the religious beliefs and give reasons *why* people adopt the commitments they hold, one implicitly acknowledges that one or more of the genetic theories of religion may be valid. If one says, like Wittgenstein, that the *reason* why people adopt, say, Christian ethics, is because they think it is true, then this cuts off questions about arbitrariness. In the believer's eyes, any theory which simply gave an account of the origin of belief in terms of psychological needs, etc., would falsify the essential character of the belief for him. On this view, religious beliefs are only arbitrary in the sense that dancing for joy is an arbitrary activity. If asked why they do this, the answer is they do, that is all. It seems to be part of the Wittgensteinian view that there must always be the appearance of arbitrariness about moral or religious beliefs where they are correctly understood as expressions of value. They only appear to be arbitrary to someone who assumes that they must have *grounds* and be subject to *explanation*.

Malcolm relates an incident which illustrates Wittgenstein's impatience with the idea that religion rests on a *rational* foundation: 'When I once quoted to him a remark of Kierkegaard's to this effect: "How can it be that Christ does not exist, since I know that He has saved me?", Wittgenstein exclaimed: "You see! It isn't a question of *proving* anything!" '[75] If the term 'Christ' in this quotation refers to a person who actually lived, rather than a symbol representing the values of the Christian faith, then one is bound to find

[74] *Letters and Papers from Prison* (Fontana, 1965), p. 123.
[75] *Memoir*, p. 71.

the statement puzzling. From one point of view, it makes a perfectly legitimate comment on the integrity of religious faith. To use Wittgenstein's own terms, the 'indubitability' of the historic basis to the faith 'wouldn't be enough to make me change my whole life'.[76] If the reason for adopting the religious beliefs is merely because certain historical facts are indubitably true, then the religious worth of the choice falls outside the quality of genuinely religious faith. From another point of view the comment is less satisfactory. Is it necessary for the believer to *assume* that the values which now dominate his life were actually embodied in flesh and blood, in one Jew say, or a group within the Jewish nation, etc.? Would the values be *religious* values if it was discovered that events traditionally associated with the 'genesis' of these values never actually took place? Christian faith does not 'rest' on a historic basis in the sense that the indubitability of the facts is a reason for adopting the faith, but does it not 'rest' on a historic basis in the sense that its intelligibility depends upon the fact that a bare minimum of its foundational events took place?

The question of the place of historical beliefs in the Wittgensteinian approach is yet another aspect of its apparent arbitrariness. In the Wittgensteinian scheme truth is a context-dependent notion. To discover the appropriate meaning of truth in relation to religious belief, one must look to that context. As we have seen, for philosophers like Phillips, 'truth' in the religious context is used of a belief or set of beliefs by which one can live, receive sustenance from, and assess one's life and all the events which shape it: 'In morality and religion truth is a personal matter'.[77] To take an example from the moral sphere; consider the belief that it is better to give than to receive. If someone responds by saying, 'There's a lot of truth in that,' then this is analogous to what is meant by saying that a religious belief

[76] L.C., p. 57.
[77] C.P., p. 150.

is true. One cannot argue for the truth of generosity in the way that one may argue about statements of fact, hypotheses, predictions, etc. I have argued that the Wittgensteinians are not necessarily offering a relativistic notion of 'true'. That is, they are not using 'true' in the sense of 'true for a particular group'. They are rejecting any general notion of truth which depends upon an external test to give confirmation or disconfirmation in every case. The question I raised in the last paragraph, however, asks whether there is not *one* sense in which beliefs introduce a 'public' notion of truth when we assume their dependence upon historical events.

Wittgenstein made the following comment in *On Certainty* about the general issue here:

> The reason why the use of the expression 'true or false' has something misleading about it is that it is like saying 'it tallies with the facts or it doesn't', and the very thing that is in question is what 'tallying' is here.[78]

The 'tallying' which I have in mind in the present context is not any pedantic notion which is sometimes found in dogmatic or sceptical views of religious beliefs in the insistence that religious doctrines must correspond with historical facts. Rather, I am asking how the religious values which the Wittgensteinians stress 'tally' with the primary events of the faith in a way which does not make the religious beliefs appear as 'timeless' ideas and ideals. A specific example will probably best explain what I have in mind. Socrates had an *absolute* confidence in the fact that a good man cannot be harmed—even in Athens:

> *Callicles*: You seem to me, Socrates, as confident that none of these things will happen to you as if you were living in another world and were not liable to be dragged into court, possibly by some scoundrel of the vilest character.
> *Socrates*: I should be a fool, Callicles, if I didn't realize that in this state anything may happen to anybody . . .

[78]   O.C., 199.

> *Callicles*: Do you really think, Socrates, that all is well with a man in such a position who cannot defend himself before his country?
>
> *Socrates*: I do think so, Callicles, provided that he has at his disposal the form of self-defence whose strength you have yourself frequently acknowledged, the defence which consists in never having committed an offence against God or man either in word or deed.[79]

Socrates' confidence here is *absolute* in the sense that it is not dependent upon anything that may happen. A person may affirm the same kind of belief that we see expressed by Socrates here and the belief would be true if the above dialogue had never taken place. Yet, one of the things which distinguishes Christianity as a religion is the close relation between Christian beliefs and an historical figure, Jesus of Nazareth.

It is not difficult to see how questions about historical facts would be quite inconsequential for the kind of view of religious belief advocated in R. B. Braithwaite's *An Empiricist's View of the Nature of Religious Belief*.[80] For Braithwaite, the stories of the New Testament are *psychological aids* towards the living of a moral life. That is, the *content* of a moral intention is independent of the Christian stories. But the Wittgensteinian approach should not be confused with Braithwaite's. For Phillips, religious beliefs are *themselves the expression* of a moral vision. Therefore, the 'historical' events of Christianity are internally related to the beliefs for Phillips in a way which they are not for Braithwaite. For the latter, if certain pictures, stories, etc., were judged to be ineffectual in the living out of a believer's moral vision, then a different set of stories, etc., could be chosen. The new stories may be successful as aids, to a greater or lesser degree than previously, but the moral vision would be essentially the same. Not so for Phillips;

---

[79] Plato, *Gorgias* (Penguin Books, 1973 ed.), pp. 139–41.
[80] Basil Mitchell (ed.) *The Philosophy of Religion* (O.U.P., 1971), pp. 72–91.

different pictures would constitute another moral vision. It is *how* this vision—the Christian one—is related to its foundational events which is difficult to grasp in the Wittgensteinian approach.

When Wittgenstein discusses the question of belief and historical events in *Lectures and Conversations*, he is anxious to stress that believers do not treat their faith as a matter of *reasonability*, as though it depended on some 'criterion of reliability'.[81] He claims that believers do not apply the 'doubt which would ordinarily apply to *any* historical propositions'.[82] If we claim that religious beliefs do not depend on the reliability of reports about the life of one man, Jesus, what are we claiming? Are we saying that the values are true in themselves—like Socrates' belief—and that it does not matter whether the familiar events which surround the story of Jesus' life ever took place? Or are we saying that while we *may* doubt some historical propositions—about Napoleon and so on—we could *never* doubt the events on which our faith was based? If the former is the case, it is difficult to distinguish Christianity from timeless ideas and ideals, and it goes against a very strong strand in Christianity which has stressed the 'scandal of particularity'—that the Word became flesh and not an idea or an ideal. If the latter is the case, we should have to explain why the findings of scholars and historians are apparently ruled out as inconsequential in principle. The absence of a full discussion of the historical dimension of religious belief from the Wittgensteinian writings makes it difficult to resolve these questions. This might be evidence for some that the Wittgensteinians, in fact, are not discussing religion as believers understand it. This leads us on to the fourth question I mooted at the beginning of this chapter, the question of reductionism in the Wittgensteinian approach. This is the subject of the next chapter.

81 *L.C.*, pp. 57–8.
82 *L.C.*, p. 57.

CHAPTER FIVE

The Question of Reductionism

BERNARD WILLIAMS has suggested a criterion for testing whether it is Christianity which is being believed in any particular case:

> This is that God is transcendent to human affairs and to human attitudes in a sense which has the following consequence (though it is supposed to mean more as well): that God would exist whether human beings and their attitudes existed or not—even if there were no human beings or human aspirations, there would still be a God . . . And I think it worth asking oneself very carefully when confronted with some reinterpretation of Christian doctrine whether it passes this test: that it represents God as a being who would be there even if no human beings, or indeed other finite conscious beings, were there. If it does not, then I suspect you no longer have any form of Christianity, but probably some form of religious humanism.[1]

According to this criterion, the Wittgensteinian view fails the test. But the adequacy of this kind of test is, of course, part of what the whole issue is about. Is Williams simply being 'held captive by a picture'? Is he assuming that God should be 'there' in the way the planets are 'there', i.e., by analogy with the reality of a physical object?[2] Phillips himself has argued that the believer needs to show that he has a relationship to something *other* than himself, if any sense is to be made of the notion of the grace of God, and, of course, of the idea of God itself.[3] What then is the problem? As Phillips puts it, it is the *grammar* of the concept which eludes us.[4]

[1] 'Has "God" a Meaning?' *Question* 1 1968, p. 53.
[2] See *C.P.*, p. 41.
[3] *C.P.*, pp. 68–75.
[4] *C.P.*, p. 43.

The debate about the sense of the *transcendence* of God is central in modern theology. A decade ago John A. T. Robinson popularized talk of the God 'out there' as a description of an inadequate picture which dominates men's thoughts about God. Phillips meant something similar when he picked up Wittgenstein's 'A *picture* held us captive'.[5] It should not be supposed, however, that Phillips is among those philosophers and theologians who wish to replace the image of a God 'out there' by grounding the reality of God in a different metaphysical system. A quotation from an essay by Robinson may well serve as a good contrast against which to see the character of Phillips' overall position. The essay sketches in some of the logic implicit in his more strictly theological writings:

> ... if God-statements are *only* statements about man ... if ... that language about God can be translated into language about man without remainder, then ... you've really given up talking about the reality for which the word 'God' has traditionally stood.
>
> For this reality has always been seen as that to which any human commitment and concern is simply *response*. 'God' refers not to the commitment but to something that hits you, meets you, surrounds you, with a grace and a claim from which you cannot finally get away. Consider these typical religious statements:
>
> Thus saith the Lord
>
> Abba, Father
>
> Herein is love not that we loved God, but that he first loved us
>
> These are not simply statements about human attitudes; they are responses to *how things are seen to be*, to that in which human life is grounded—viewed not simply as an impersonal regularity but as claiming one in freedom and responsibility, not simply as an 'It' but as a 'Thou'. It is *this*, as the ultimate truth about reality, that God-language is affirming.[6]

[5] See *P.I.*, 115 and *C.P.*, p. 41.
[6] J. A. T. Robinson, 'Has "God" a Meaning?' *Question* 1, 1968, pp. 58–9.

A basic difference between Robinson and Phillips is there-fore found in the former's stress on *how* things are and the latter's stress on *that* things are. Phillips appeals to the distinction between the *how* and the *that* of things in his attempt to demonstrate that prayer cannot be equated with forms of self-knowledge. The believer, says Phillips, con-templates something *other* than himself.[7] To grasp the *religious* meaning of this, one must see that the believer acknowledges that he cannot deliver himself by his own moral efforts. We learn from Phillips' exposition that what is *other* than the believer's self-knowledge is in his con-templating *that* other people are, rather than *how* they are. Phillips quotes Simone Weil: ' "Belief in the existence of human beings as such is *love*" '.[8] This recognition involves a renunciation of any 'natural' feelings about our rights and needs. It is to realize 'that nothing is ours by right, that all is given.'[9] To use the language of religion is to assent to these truths: 'To say "Thy will be done", is to accept these truths in one's soul.'[10] But is all of this an adequate account of religious belief as it is normally understood?

The question that arises is whether or not the grammar of belief is complete without the kind of considerations that J. A. T. Robinson claimed were essentials, e.g., some belief about how things are seen to be. According to Phillips religious language is adequate for its purpose. By analysing the grammar of that language we can learn what the real and the unreal amount to in that mode of discourse. There is no

---

Phillips' view is sometimes uncritically linked with Robinson's and clouds the issues at stake; see H. Meynell 'Kai Nielsen and the Concept of God' *Question* 5, 1972, pp. 48–54, and K. Nielsen 'A Reply to Hugo Meynell' *Question* 5, 1972, pp. 55–62. A similar misunderstanding of Phillips is evident when his work is bracketed with Tillich; see J. King-Farlow & W. N. Christensen, *Faith and the Life of Reason* (D. Reidel Pub. Co., Holland, 1972), pp. 94–9.

[7] *C.P.*, p. 68.
[8] *C.P.*, p. 69.
[9] *C.P.*, p. 70.
[10] *C.P.*, p. 70.

question of language *as such* being inadequate to express what is real in religion: 'Our language is not a poor alternative to other means of communication; it is what constitutes communication.'[11] The contrast with Robinson's approach could scarcely be sharper. Robinson acknowledges that the word 'God' is burdened with confusing associations. 'However,' says Robinson, 'it's the reality that I'm concerned with, not the word.'[12] Robinson implies that it is possible to conceive of the reality without the language. It is precisely this that Phillips wants to deny.

Robinson is able to speak in these terms, for religious commitment is *a response to how things are*:

> ... to believe in God is to affirm that at the heart of things, as the most real thing in the world, is a love and a purpose to which persons and personal relationships are, so far, the highest *response*. This is the way the grain of the universe runs.[13]

Although Robinson's believer may participate in religion and use its language, when he expresses a belief in how things are seen to be, it remains, as Robinson says, an act of *trust*. When Phillips' believer uses religious language there is nothing over and above this which involves an act of trust that something is so. The notion of the transcendence of God is not essentially problematical on Phillips' view; it is a matter of getting the grammar of the language right. As Phillips acknowledges, this is no easy task. Nevertheless, for Robinson, the problem of God's transcendence arises from the necessity of seeing how God transcends the realities to which, on his view, belief is a *response*.

I have mentioned Robinson's views here simply to draw up a contrast between the Wittgensteinian approach— represented by Phillips—and a standpoint which attempts to maintain a *reference* for God. I am not concerned here with the question of whether Robinson's own position is

[11] *D.I.*, p. 15.
[12] *Question* 1, 1968, p. 57.
[13] *Question* 1, 1968, p. 61.

adequate in itself, but simply with his claim that religious beliefs must be about *how things are seen to be*. This is to put the matter in a very general way. All kinds of distinctions and standpoints could be made under this bare statement of the minimal core of what makes a religious belief a religious belief, namely, in its reference to what is the case. Such distinctions would range from straightforward literal theism to the most tenuous connections with 'how things are seen to be', which is sometimes apparent in Robinson's writings. Nevertheless, all these standpoints, as diverse as they may be, have something in common when they are set over against the Wittgensteinian view in which there is no substantive reference for 'God' at all. To put the matter very crudely, down the Wittgensteinian road believers express values; down the opposite road they assert facts. One of these roads is the 'broad way' which leads to reductionism. Which one? In most theological circles the suspicion would all be on Phillips' side. Where lies the reductionism, if any?

Whatever conclusion we come to, no one can accuse Phillips of *conscious* reductionism. At no point does he put 'God' into inverted commas. Religious beliefs have a distinctive content and cannot be characterized as psychological aids, and so on. Indeed, in his various analyses Phillips is at pains to show that religious beliefs are not *other kinds* of belief in disguise; prayer cannot be equated with various forms of self-knowledge, assimilated to other forms of talking to non-language users, etc.[14] We can grasp some idea of how his own work is directed *against* reductionism by realizing that he, like Simone Weil, is critical of what the latter calls a 'natural God'.[15] Believers in the natural God commit what Phillips calls the *naturalistic fallacy* in religion, i.e., by identifying the will of God with anything natural.[16]

---

[14] *C.P.*, pp. 43; 64–75.
[15] *C.P.*, p. 98.
[16] *C.P.*, pp. 100–1; 106.

Wittgenstein had said that 'It is not *how* things are in the world that is mystical, but *that* it exists.'[17] Echoing these words, Phillips asserts that the naturalistic fallacy 'is to think that religion concerns *how* the world is.'[18] To *reduce* religion is to say that it is something it is not. Is religion basically a distinctive way of responding to the contingency of events in the world, or is it, fundamentally, trust in what is ultimately believed to be the case about the nature of the universe? If the former is the case, religious language is *expressive* and non-referential in character. If the latter is the case, religious language *refers to* something—however that 'something' may be defined. The disagreement is very deep.

A natural reaction to Phillips' case is to ask, granted there is no *reference to* 'God', what has happened to the *active* reality independent of man? If we give up trying to extract a God from nature, do we not have to say that God, to be God, must *act* in order that man may respond? I will not spend time trying to argue that the God of the Old and New Testaments is an 'active' God. It is obvious on nearly every page of the Bible that this is how God was conceived; He 'brings' a people out of Egypt and 'sends' His only Son for man's redemption. In any case, Phillips would hardly contest this. The question is how the language of God's activity is to be understood. Phillips' approach may be forceful in persuading us to see the primitive man's morning sacrifice in the context of wonder at a new day arriving, humility before the dawn, living life as a gift, and so on, rather than a piece of causal apparatus to make sure that the sun rises.[19] His view guards against reductionism in that setting, i.e., where the term 'religion' is applied to ritualistic responses to the changes of the seasons, phases of the moon, etc. But does not this same 'sympathetic' approach involve reductionism in its treatment of a major religion like Christianity?

[17] *T.*, 6.44.
[18] *C.P.*, p. 102.
[19] See *Athronyddu am Grefydd*, p. 57.

Some of Phillips' own arguments in this context have not been very helpful to his own case. For example, consider his attempts to make sense of the distinction between God's acting and refraining from acting, in the light of his own non-referential position.[20] At one point Phillips tries to show that God cannot be thought of as a 'power amongst powers' and therefore a relative reality.[21] In the course of discussing J. R. Jones' definition of the Gospel, Phillips says that the Gospel is not concerned with a higher power, but a new idea about power; namely, the ability to refrain from using it. He argues that Jesus demonstrated his divinity by refraining from using power on the Cross—he stayed there. To have stepped down from the Cross would have made him a power amongst powers.[22] In order to make his point here Phillips unconsciously relies on a factual interpretation in order to establish a significant contrast between the ability to exercise and refrain from a use of power. But the implication of Phillips' position elsewhere is that Jesus possessed no such power to step from the Cross. There was no Heavenly Father to facilitate the descent.

Phillips goes on[23] to ask whether Jesus' act of powerlessness on the Cross is not the divine call to the Christian to refrain from the powers which are *naturally* his. But, as we have seen, Jesus possessed no such *natural* power to descend from the Cross. Jesus no doubt had the power to refrain from despair or bitter recrimination. This could be 'divine' inspiration for Christians. But this is not what Phillips is claiming. Phillips needs something to explain how God can *refrain* from using power when, on his own view, it is confused to think that God is the kind of reality who *could* use the power which would deny His divinity.

[20] See R. W. Hepburn's comments in his review of Phillips' *The Concept of Prayer*, *Philosophical Books*, May 1966, Vol. VII No. 2, pp. 24–5.
[21] See Phillips' essay 'Yr Argyfwng Gwacter Ystyr' (1965) ('The Crisis of the Emptiness of Meaning') in *Athronyddu am Grefydd*, esp. pp. 82–3.
[22] Ibid., p. 82.
[23] Ibid., p. 83.

I will not discuss this difficulty any further here. I simply mention the problem as one which needs to be more carefully grappled with by the Wittgensteinians. It need not be an insurmountable difficulty. Just because the language of 'activity' is used of God in the Bible does not *in itself* show that the users of the language thought that they were referring to an *agent* who acted independently of themselves. It is always possible to ask what this language *means*.

There are, no doubt, many other questions we could raise about the question of reductionism in the Wittgensteinian view. However, I shall confine myself to one main problem for the remainder of this chapter. If we set aside for the moment the problem of the sense of God's activity, is there not one sense, at least, in which the religious believer *must* believe that someone or something independent of himself *acted*? That is, is it not essential to religious belief that it provides some explanation for the very existence of the world? Is it not the height of reductionism to be indifferent to *this* question? Let us ask what is involved is these questions.

To put the matter very simply, on the Wittgensteinian view the world is 'given' and there is no substantive 'giver'. Yet, are we not entitled to ask where the world came from? Many people would say that a religious belief could not be a *religious* belief if it made no provision for this question. It is true that religions of all kinds have usually provided believers with an idea of *where* the world came from, of *how* to live now, and to *what* the whole process is leading. In the Christian scheme, God created the world and will be 'all in all' at the consummation of history. Christians live 'between the times'. Christian theologians have often spoken of the events traditionally associated with the beginning and the end as symbolic material projected into the past and future respectively to express the single truth of man's dependence on God. They have done so, however, while attempting to retain the idea of God as a substantive reality. That is, the 'events' do not refer to any real event as we understand the word. How could they? Yet the theologians insist on saying that 'God' is not a symbolic way of talking about human attitudes, whether we call them 'secular' or 'religious'. We must, therefore, distinguish the Wittgensteinian approach from the common theological treatment of the origin of the world as symbolic which nevertheless retains a *reference* for God.

'Where does the world come from?' What are we to make of this question after listening to the Wittgensteinian analysis? It is an important question because, naïve as it may sound, it does point to a great difficulty experienced by many people who read the Wittgensteinians.[24]

We are frequently reminded by Phillips that we do violence to religious beliefs if we import any notion of factual reference. The beliefs are expressions of values, the frameworks within which the believer lives his life. Similarly, 'God' is not a metaphysical notion of any kind. The world requires no such super-fact to explain it and, in any case, such a notion plays no part in religious belief itself. The world is *given* and provides the setting for religious belief.

Although the belief in God as the *source* of the world has been expressed in different ways down the centuries, most people would assume that without this belief, in some form, religion would be a secondary thing. Hence the question: 'Where does the world come from?' Phillips' most direct treatment of this question is in an essay, 'From World to God?'[25] He brings out many of the logical points made by Rhees.[26] The latter draws attention to the *grammar* of what we call 'explaining how something came to exist'. His general point is that you cannot pass straight from questions about the origin or existence of particular things to questions about the origin of 'the world', 'everything' or 'reality'.[27] Of the existence of a *particular* thing we are able to say 'it might not

[24] Rhees has considered the question briefly in *Without Answers*, pp. 115f.
[25] *F.P.E.*, pp. 35–61.
[26] *Without Answers*, pp. 115f.
[27] Ibid., pp. 115–19.

have existed', and we can raise the question of how it came into existence. This question, however, can only be answered by reference to other things which actually *do* exist.[28]

Phillips has these grammatical difficulties in mind when he attempts to analyse the sense of talking of God as the *source* of the world. The difficulties are there whether we regard the world, or 'everything', as a 'class of things' or as a 'thing': 'the notion of class entails the notion of a limit, and a distinction between things inside and outside the limit. But when we speak of things being in the world, we do not mean to contrast them with other things which are outside the world.'[29] Similar difficulties are involved in thinking of the world as a thing:

> Has the world the unity of an object? If it has, it ought to be possible to identify the world demonstratively. In order to do so, however, we should have to determine that the world is the thing it is and not another thing. Any object or group of objects is individuated against a background of other objects. But against what background do we individuate the world? If 'everything' is thought to be a thing, we cannot answer the question, '*This* thing as distinct from what?'[30]

Phillips therefore sees a logical difficulty in a certain way of speaking of God as the source of the world. He cannot see what is meant by saying that there is something other than the world.[31] However, Phillips does not wish to conclude that belief in God as the source of the world is meaningless.[32] He finds a remedy in taking the question '*Why* is there anything at all?' to mean 'What is the *sense* of it?'[33] 'When someone asks,' says Phillips, 'why there is anything at all, he need not be asking for the details of any process or development. His question may be about the sense, meaning, or reality of

28 Ibid., pp. 116f.
29 F.P.E., p. 41.
30 F.P.E., p. 42.
31 F.P.E., p. 44.
32 F.P.E., p. 46.
33 *Without Answers*, p. 119.

everything.'[34] But Phillips realizes that this way of posing the question is not without its difficulties: 'But what are we asking for when we ask for the meaning of everything? If we want to give an adequate explanation of the meaning of *this*, we must refer to something *other than this*. But if we ask for the meaning of everything, what can we refer to which is other than everything?'[35] Phillips works around this problem by arguing that this difficulty is only insuperable if we try to locate the meaning of the world *outside* the world.[36] He believes that we can speak of a meaning of the world which is not *outside* the world but which may be regarded as *other* than the world in order to preserve the essentially religious distinction between God and the world. As we saw in an earlier chapter, Phillips draws this distinction by contrasting the *eternal* view—dying to the world's way of regarding things—with the *temporal* view—seeing 'objects as it were from the midst of them'.

The thrust of Phillips' analysis is to suggest that the question 'Where does the world come from?' does not make sense if it anticipates a certain kind of answer. If our question expects some kind of *explanation*, then it is confused. The question makes sense if it is an *expression* of thanks that the world should be at all. Rhees has an important passage which underlies Phillips' analysis:

> Do I mean that people who ask what brought the world into being are just confused and deluded, then?
>
> No, but I think the sense is different from this quasi physical one.
>
> The question is much more '*Why* is there anything at all? What is the sense of it?'
>
> Or it may be an expression of wonder at the world. ('Isn't it extraordinary that anything at all should exist?') Which easily passes into reverence at the wonder of it—the wonder at there

---

[34] *F.P.E.*, p. 47.
[35] *F.P.E.*, p. 48.
[36] *F.P.E.*, p. 48.

being anything at all. There is gratitude in this too—gratitude for the existence of things.[37]

Rhees' remarks are closely related to Wittgenstein's wonder at the existence of the world in his lecture on ethics and his references to the mystical in the *Tractatus*. Rhees thinks that this way of expressing the matter moves us away from expecting a *causative* answer to the question 'Where does the world come from?' But does it not take us towards another way of 'individuating' the world in the sense demanded by Phillips' analysis? That is, if we wonder at the existence of the world, do we ask why there is something *rather than nothing*? Does 'nothing' or 'non-being' provide us with the background against which we can individuate the world?[38] J. R. Jones, in fact, pursued this line of thought in Tillichian terms.[39] Phillips criticizes Jones' analysis.[40] He challenges Jones' changing of Wittgenstein's phrase 'How extraordinary that anything should exist?' into Heidegger's 'Why is there being and not nothing?' The creatures can wonder, says Phillips, at the fact that there is anything at all. This wonder can naturally be transformed into a feeling of thankfulness. But it is not wonder at the fact that there is something *rather than nothing*. It is wonder *at* existence.[41] For Phillips, there is no need to bring in the 'cloudy' idea of 'non-being' or 'being' as if it is something that enables particular things to be.[42]

In another article, J. R. Jones admits the force of Phillips' criticism of the Tillichian ontology but wishes to hold on to a sense in which a person may wonder at the fact that there is

[37] *Without Answers*, p. 119.
[38] M. K. Munitz has provided a thorough study of the philosophical problems surrounding the question, 'Why does the world exist?'; *The Mystery of Existence* (Appleton-Century-Crofts, New York, 1965).
[39] J. R. Jones, 'Gwirionedd ac Ystyr' (Truth and Meaning) in *Saith Ysgrif ar Grefydd*, pp. 51–68.
[40] 'Gwirionedd, Ystyr a Chrefydd' (Truth, Meaning and Religion), *Diwinyddiaeth*, 1969, No. XX., pp. 3–18.
[41] Ibid., p. 10.
[42] Ibid., p. 10.

something *rather* than nothing. Jones claims that 'non-being' may be experienced when we feel our own nearness to being nothing, that is, the approach of death and the knowledge that the world was there before we were born and will be there when we have gone. Jones agrees, however, that the idea of 'nothing' or 'non-being' becomes confused when it is considered outside the *experience* of being grasped by the wonder of existence.[43] Outside the grip of the experience we try to catch hold of it objectively and it falls to pieces on the grammar of the word 'nothing'. This word cannot be used except in contrast with its opposite and is easily subject to logical ridicule, as Elmer Sprague shows.[44] Therefore, even Jones' retention of some sense of non-being, the wonder at the existence of the world, cannot support, for the Wittgensteinians, the kind of ontology found in the writings of Paul Tillich. The latter's attempt to speak about God in a non-objectifying way has affinities with the Wittgensteinian approach, but his reliance on the idea of 'Being' rules out a closer unity in the two standpoints.

The ideas of 'being' and 'non-being' are notoriously difficult to discuss sensibly, and there is no space here to dilate on their significance for the present study. Most of the writers who use the terms relate them closely to human experiences, like those of anxiety and the sense of finitude. 'Being' and 'non-being' abstracted from human experience become the logical jokes they are thought to be by Phillips and Sprague. Jones is more sensitive to the human significance of these notions, but his basic Wittgensteinian standpoint rules out any idea of their ultimate ground in a metaphysical sense.[45]

[43] 'Ontoleg Ffydd' (The Ontology of Faith) *Diwinyddiaeth*, 1969, No. XX, pp. 19–34, esp. pp. 26f.

[44] 'On Professor Tillich's Ontological Question' *International Philosophical Quarterly*, 1962, No. 2, pp. 81–91.

[45] J. R. Jones' Wittgensteinian standpoint is very evident in his sermon 'Love as Perception of Meaning' *Religion and Understanding*, ed. D. Z. Phillips (Blackwell, 1967), pp. 141–53.

'Being' and 'non-being', as dubious as they are as ideas, point to something of fundamental importance when they are given expression by philosophers, novelists, theologians, and so on. When believers use these ideas they are often attempting to express the sense in which God is *more* substantial than the world. Whatever the worth of the religious values on Phillips' view, some believers are bound to think that their beliefs are being classified as a product of the world, 'human religion', and so on. That is, if there never was a transcendent reality, God, who acted in history and revealed Himself to His people, did not the religious values come through a growing *human* awareness? Do we have *creative interpretations* and not *interventions* of a transcendent reality? Is not man the creative source of his own religious values and meanings, as philosophers like Nietzsche and Sartre have always urged? These are the questions that are bound to arise in the minds of some believers in the light of the Wittgensteinian analysis. These questions express the fear that there is reductionism at the heart of the Wittgensteinians' interpretation—the reduction of the reality of 'God' to merely *human* concerns. I think, however, that this objection is unfair to Wittgenstein and his followers. It is a natural objection but too crude to be very informative.

The Wittgensteinian approach, as we have found it expressed in Phillips' work, has both a positive and a negative side which must be recognized before we rashly classify it as reductionism or disguised atheism. The positive side comes out in the stress on the distinctively *religious* content of beliefs. The Wittgensteinians are concerned with *language*, it is true. But they are far from reducing the language of religious beliefs to the language of the realities which are presupposed by those beliefs, e.g., sentient beings, the natural world, etc. Thus they are *against* reductionism in their efforts to show that religious beliefs are not *other* kinds of belief in disguise. They may succeed in this to greater or lesser degrees; it would be up to other people to offer better analyses. The negative side is perhaps best appreciated by a comment from Wittgenstein: 'A *picture* held us captive. And we could not get outside of it, for it lay in our language and language seemed to repeat it to us inexorably.'[46] Wittgenstein refers here to the captivating hold of a fundamental idea of the *Tractatus*: 'The general form of propositions is: This is how things are.'[47] If we apply the same metaphor of a captivating picture to the language of religion, we can grasp much that lies behind Phillips' programme of work. We are captivated by the idea that religious language refers to something, that 'God' is an entity of some kind, and so on. The tendency to suppose that this must be so is one of the deep roots in language. As we saw in Chapter Two, Wittgenstein describes his own method as bringing 'words back from their metaphysical to their everyday use'.[48] In a similar way, Phillips attempts to do this in his analysis of religious belief. When religious beliefs are taken as metaphysical systems or epistemological theories, they have strayed from their 'everyday use' in the religious sphere. The fact that the charge of reductionism is made when the captivating hold of this picture is broken may be an index of just how seductive the picture is—'it lay in our language and language seemed to repeat it to us inexorably'. Phillips deliberately intends that the metaphysical dimension should go and this is probably the chief source of the charge of reductionism.

If there is atheism is Phillips' work, it is a *metaphysical atheism*. Phillips is an 'atheist' in the sense that his analyses deny a concept of 'God' which includes the idea that 'God' refers to something which is 'there' whether people believe in Him or not. It is arguable, at least, that there have been anti-metaphysical believers of great stature in the religious tradition. For example, consider one of Simone Weil's

[46] P.I., 115.
[47] P.I., 114; see T., 4.5.
[48] P.I., 116.

sayings—for Phillips, one of her greatest sayings—about the transcendence of God's 'presence' in the world: 'God can only be present in creation under the form of absence.'[49] The *absence* of God is His *mode of appearing*. We cannot, of course, interpret this to mean that God was once present to the senses but is now not so. From the Wittgensteinian perspective to say that God is *absent* is not to imply that he is present elsewhere. The words of Simone Weil do not imply anything about the location or being of God in any sense. Rather, the saying is about the transparency of the believer's life to the necessary scrutiny of the 'eternal' view. It is the 'natural' God who is absent—the God of compensations who is important to the believer who thinks that things must go one way rather than another.

To keep the Wittgensteinian view in a proper perspective we should remind ourselves that most of the writings we have discussed are concerned with the *philosophy of* religion. Phillips, for example, is not writing as a theologian, a fideist, etc. Thus, from one point of view, he is simply saying that there is a use of religious language, an *expressive* use, which has been badly neglected by philosophers, a use which does not fit the canons of rationality which are usually brought to bear on religious belief. However, Phillips seems to assume that the kind of religion which is given expression in this neglected use is also *genuine* religion. This is much more controversial. It has implications not only for what philosophers and theologians have said at a second order about the *grammar* of first order religious language, but also about the levels of authentic and inauthentic religion in the scriptures and the tradition itself.

This issue is more complex than the last paragraph might suggest. Philosophers or theologians might assume, as most of them in fact do, that religious language must have a referential grammar, i.e., the language *refers to* something

---

[49]   *Gravity and Grace*, p. 99; see Phillips' comment in *Saith Ysgrif ar Grefydd*, p. 134.

outside the language itself. Phillips is arguing that they are mistaken. But further, Phillips' position implies that some uses of first order religious language positively invite a referential grammar. Thus, where God is spoken of as a power superior to, but on the same level as, all other powers, He becomes a kind of super-fact. Or, again, while St Paul may be arguing (in 1 Corinthians 15) the case for the resurrected body in factual and discredited metaphysical terms, what he says elsewhere about 'dying daily' (Romans 6 and 1 Corinthians 15:31) may express true religion which does not invite a referential grammar. I will say a little more about this in the next chapter. We could conclude the present discussion by saying that the Wittgensteinian analyses do not 'reduce' religion to something it is not. Rather, they draw attention to one kind of religious belief which does not fall victim to sceptical philosophy. Perhaps they aim to do no more than this.

CHAPTER SIX

The Possibilities in the Language

THE GREAT majority of philosophers of religion—whatever their own religious position—insist that religious language must at least claim to have some kind of factual reference. Not surprisingly there is something of a 'gap' separating them from the Wittgensteinians. John Hick has referred to this feature of contemporary philosophy of religion and leaves us in no doubt about where his loyalties lie:

> To those of us on the other side of the gap it seems possible for two people genuinely to differ, in a common language, about what the character of the universe is, and about whether or not its ultimate determining factor is the eternal personal reality which theistic religion calls God. In other words, it seems to us that the question of the existence of God is a real, and in a broad sense of the word a factual, question.[1]

Hick's own work, in fact, together with that of philosophers like the late Ian T. Ramsey, is representative of a very different response to contemporary empiricism compared with that found in Phillips' writings. Phillips has resisted the practice of foisting certain ideas of reasonableness, rationality, etc., upon religion in the spirit of an uncritical empiricism. By contrast, Hick and Ramsey attempt to *enlarge* our ideas of reasonableness, and so on, in an attempt to show how the term 'God' does, in a broad sense, have a factual reference.

Hick and Ramsey differ between themselves in their empirical approaches. For Hick, the facts of our experience are ambiguous and capable of more than one interpretation. But for Ramsey the datum is not neutral. There are certain

---

[1] Hick's review of S. C. Brown's *Do Religious Claims Make Sense?* (S.C.M., 1969) in *Philosophical Books*, May 1970, Vol. XI No. 2, p. 4.

facts about diety—disclosed facts—and a world-view which ignores them is inadequate. That is, there is a special kind of unobservable datum which is missed by a narrow or 'unbelieving' empiricism. Hick insists on the 'cognitive' status of religious belief and Ramsey stresses the need to preserve what he calls the 'objective' reference of Christian assertions. Despite the different ways of posing the problem, they are united in their insistence upon the fact that religious language *refers*: 'Somewhere or other they (i.e. Christian assertions) must encourage us to appeal to "what is the case".'[2]

There is no space here to discuss whether Hick's or Ramsey's own attempts succeed in making their point. I simply mention their views to give some indication of just how deep the disagreement is between the rival views of the nature of religious grammar. There is, of course, no *neutral* procedure for settling which side is right. Both sides express the nature of the problem in quite different terms. Up to this point the issue has been discussed as a problem in the philosophy of religion. It may, however, be of equal significance for theology itself. There must clearly be a close connection between the philosopher's subject matter and the tradition which the theologian expounds. It may well be that the 'mental cramps' which bedevil modern theology may be eased by paying closer attention to the grammar of its presuppositions. The contemporary theological issues will appear differently depending upon whether the theologian sees his subject matter as *lying beyond*, or as *expressed through*, its language.

The Possibilities in the Language

The Wittgensteinian view I have examined sees religious language as *expressive* in character and one which offers

---

[2] I. T. Ramsey, *Models for Divine Activity*, p. 58; see Hick's *God and the Universe of Faiths*, p. vii.

people possibilities of meaning for their lives. The language gives expression to religious 'pictures' which form the whole framework for the believer's life. The 'pictures' are not substitutes for anything more substantial than themselves. If they die, something irreplaceable dies with them. At the present time in the Western world religious pictures are losing their hold on many people's lives. There are many reasons for this. If the social, political and economic life of man changes, we must expect to see changes in the possibilities for meaning which it offers. Language is not something which is simply *added* to social life to facilitate communication; it is *itself* the embodiment of these possibilities. Life and language may change in such a way that older ways of living and expression are put under pressure and may lose their hold altogether; '. . . new types of language, new language-games, as we may say, come into existence, and others become obsolete and get forgotten.'[3]

If this is true, what happens to religious forms of expression in a period of rapid change? Changes are not necessarily inimical of religion, but there are strong reasons for thinking that today religion is becoming less and less of a *possibility* for people. Not only may people find that religion now provides only a very alien way of being human, contemporary forms of language make it difficult for people who are religious to give expression to this in their own lives. Where the language of fact has a culturally privileged status,[4] an expressive language, if it survives, will come to be regarded as a cumbersome way of saying what could be said more directly, or as a language which is simply false. If language is seen solely as that which *refers to something else*, a

[3] P.I., 23.
[4] Theodore Roszak's *Where the Wasteland Ends* (Faber & Faber, London, 1973) is typical of present day laments of the consequences of the reductionist pressure of science. In *Theological Explorations* (S.C.M., London, 1968) we find a contrite Paul van Buren: 'we modern theologians are all too modern . . . and therefore too literal, too prosaic, too unimaginative. We are accepting too uncritically the culturally privileged status of the language of factuality, explanation' etc. (p. 180).

genuinely expressive language will seem to be expressing nothing at all. If religious beliefs are an example of an expressive language, religion will appear as superstition in such a time.[5] That is, the language will survive without the forms of social life which nourish it and make it *religious* language.

There may have been a time, say, two thousand years ago in Palestine, when a religious response to life was the only *possibility* in the language of that culture. Even the 'fool' of Psalm 14 must be seen as the unrighteous man who *defies* God, rather than as a theoretical atheist.[6] Atheism as *we* know it did not have a language then and in that place. Are we approaching a time which is an exact reversal of that old situation? We may be, but we are not there yet. Ian Robinson raises a question which is vital to what I have just said. In a chapter called 'Religious English', he raises the question of whether modern English is a *serious* enough language to give expression to religious beliefs, liturgies, biblical translations, etc. Showing no mercy to its translators, Robinson attempts to show how the language of fact has actually taken over in the *New English Bible*. The very language which has put religious language under pressure is adopted as the language for holy writ. Robinson tries to demonstrate that a failure in *style* is also a failure in *meaning* and *content*:[7]

> The N.E.B. version of the New Testament records a mean, insignificant religious movement . . . In the N.E.B. Satan tries to establish a feudal system with Jesus as a vassal, but Jesus says, after the manner of the Victorian damsel rebuking the importunate villain, 'Begone Satan!' . . . A similar girlish gush ends the first chapter of the Sermon on the Mount: 'You must

---

[5] Roszak speaks of the religion of the minimal God who 'lingers on like a fond old relative who has been so expertly embalmed' (Ibid., p. 186).

[6] In a fascinating essay, O. K. Bouwsma gives a Wittgensteinian interpretation of Anselm's Argument in terms of the language of praise and contrasts the 'literate' fool of Anselm's proof with the fool of the Psalm; 'Anselm's Argument' in J. Bobik (ed.), *The Nature of Philosophical Enquiry* (Univ. of Notre Dame Press, 1970), pp. 252–93.

[7] *The Survival of English*, pp. 35 & 41.

therefore be all goodness, just as your heavenly Father is all good' . . . There is also something very Victorian-governessy here: 'Then I will tell them to their face, "I never knew you: out of my sight, you and your wicked ways!" '[8]

Robinson thinks that an alternative to the language of the 'slangy crib' we are offered in the N.E.B. would have been a language which does for our day what the Bible English did for the readers of the old version, i.e., a modern religious English.[9] The problem is where the latter is to come from. Robinson's complaint against the N.E.B. translators, however, is not that they did not find one, but that the problem apparently never occurred to them. A group of writers who do seem to be sensitive to the problem have contributed to a book called *The Prose For God*.[10] Their concern is perhaps best conveyed by the epigraph from which the title is taken:

> *Trebell* . . . I'm offering you the foundation of a New Order of men and women who'll serve God by teaching His children. Now shall we finish the conversation in prose?
> *Cantelupe* (not to be put down) What is the prose for God?
> *Trebell* (not to be put down either) That's what we irreligious people are giving our lives to discover.
>
> —Harley Granville-Barker, *Waste* (1909).[11]

Most of the contributors to *The Prose For God* appear to be united in the conviction that our *way of speaking* is inseparably connected with *what is being spoken about*. I mention this collection of essays simply to show that there are some people writing on the fate of an expressive language in our culture who are not necessarily doing so from a consciously Wittgensteinian standpoint.[12] Both *The Prose For God* and

8   Ibid., p. 35.
9   Ibid., p. 43.
10 I. Gregor & W. Stein (eds.) (Sheed & Ward, London, 1973).
11 *The Prose for God*, p. viii.
12 Cf. J. M. Cameron's comment: 'How richly the human imagination moves in that part of Europe where the enlightenment was not a deep experience, and how tenacious a hold is kept upon the modes of religious discourse, can be seen, to choose the mountainous cases, in the work of

Robinson's *The Survival of English* raise, by implication, the question of the possibility or impossibility of a contemporary syntax for 'God'. 'Yahweh'—and all that it expressed—was a word which came readily to the lips of Hebrew people two to three thousand years ago. It was a mythology, if you like, which lay heavily upon their language. Matter-of-fact language seems to dominate our culture as much as an expressive God-language dominated that of the Hebrews. But not quite. There are *residual* mythologies still left in our language. We talk about '*fate* taking a hand' or of '*luck* being with us' or something as 'having a *soul*', and so on. In none of these cases is there a literal reference to a substance or a thing. They are expressions which come naturally in certain situations. Yet we could hardly say that these kinds of 'mythologies' are pervasive or rich enough to form a body of expressive language in a sense comparable to the hold religious language once had.

The natural reaction to a breakdown in the power of traditional religious language is to ask for a new one. Recent theologies have been concerned with speaking in a 'secular way about God', the 'secular meaning of the Gospel', etc. What does this kind of talk amount to in the present context? It could mean many things, but there are at least two levels to the issue. Firstly, the plea for religion to be understood in a *secular* way may involve the assumption that the *meaning* of religion is being obscured by its traditional language and concepts, and that the new *secular* language will be a better vehicle to convey the meaning. On this view, language is one thing and meaning is another. The second level is this. The attempt to discover a *secular* meaning for the Gospel may arise from a desire to see what a contem-

---

Dostoevsky and Pasternak. Such reverberations cannot be commanded by even the greatest novelists in the West.' Cameron makes this observation after noting the deliquesence of theological language and the way in which men's minds and imaginations 'have been flattened and sand-papered by the agencies of culture since the enlightenment.' (*The Prose For God*, p. 5).

porary development of genuine religion amounts to. If this question is asked in a Wittgensteinian spirit, there cannot be the same separation between meaning and language. The task then becomes one of looking for activities, concepts and a language recognizably continuous with the genuine core of the tradition. On this second level, the important concern is the preservation and development of what is irreducibly part of the essence of the tradition, 'true religion', or however we care to put it. It may acknowledge that the cultural context is 'secular', but it resolutely refuses to compromise the truth of the tradition. In one sense, therefore, there can be no *secular* meaning of the Gospel. It must always have a *religious* meaning, although its life-setting at any particular point may be radically secular.

There is an objection to this second-level way of putting the problem. What if the character of contemporary secular society has ruled out the very possibility of viewing—what the Wittgensteinians might call—'true religion' in the old way? Does this mean that there is no point in trying to re-express the truths of religion because there are simply no amenable concepts available? I do not think our culture has quite reached this point of development, and these questions are therefore highly speculative. Nevertheless, we have to recognize a certain fatality about the Wittgensteinian view; if religious pictures decline, something *irreplaceable* dies with them. There *may* come a time when the prevailing culture makes it impossible to draw central religious distinctions between the temporal and the eternal, the way of immanence and the way of transcendence, etc.[13]

Some of the issues I have discussed here bear a striking similarity to some of the problems which concerned Matthew Arnold at the end of the nineteenth century. In

[13] For this distinction see Alistair Kee's *The Way of Transcendence* (Penguin Books, 1971). D. Z. Phillips occasionally refers in an illuminating way to the impossibility of making sense of religious beliefs in a 'Brave New World' kind of society, e.g., 'Moral Presuppositions and Literary Criticism' *The Human World*, Feb. 1972 No. 6, pp. 24-34.

Literature and Dogma and later in *God and the Bible* Arnold argued that the language of the Bible was 'literary' rather than 'scientific'. That is to say, the language of religion was not about a metaphysical entity named 'God'. One passage, in fact, is very much in sympathy with the Wittgensteinian approach which emerged a hundred years later: 'For the thing turns upon understanding the manner in which men have thought, their way of using words, and what they mean by them.'[14]

John Coulson has recently observed that although Arnold was not himself a theologian, he discussed the theological problems on which the professional theologians should have concentrated.[15] For Arnold, there was something about religious language which resists complete translation into the secular. The Wittgensteinian view I have discussed may throw some fresh light on Arnold's problems. He spoke of the religious man as one trapped between two worlds; 'one dead, the other powerless to be born'. In different terms we could say that many 'religious' people are left with a dead religious vocabulary with no prospect of a new one emerging which would contain the genuinely religious values—a world powerless to be born. The strength of religion, said Arnold, was its 'unconscious poetry'. It is precisely this which appears to be in decline today. There is the language of *Aberglaube* (Arnold's term for 'superstition') which 'materializes' the poetry, but very little of the language which could be the bearer of religious values. In his own writings, Arnold often substituted the phrase 'the Eternal' for 'God' and spoke of the reality expressed by the term as 'a power not ourselves making for righteousness'. This was simply his own attempt to describe the kind of reality God has without inviting an object-like interpretation.[16] But, as Arnold would no doubt have said, theologians

14 *Literature and Dogma* (Smith, Elder, London, 1900), p. 39.
15 *The Prose For God*, 'The Adjectives for God', pp. 41f.
16 *Literature and Dogma*, p. 47.

cannot manufacture unconscious poetry. It grows and dies. By definition, it must be a language which people may 'relax' into using.

It is unlikely that a thorough study of Arnold's works would solve our problems. His substitution of 'Eternal' for 'God' was part of Arnold's attempt to bring out the force which a word like 'God' or 'Lord' had for the Hebrews. He admits that 'Eternal' has 'less of particularity and palpability for the imagination' than a word like 'Lord'.[17] Indeed, first order religious language has to be 'consecrated by use and religious feeling' and cannot be invented *ad hoc* by individuals. As Coulson suggests, Arnold's long-term recommendation for living with our problem would be to 'return to our great religious text—the Bible—and read it with a proper attention to the literary qualities of scriptural language. Our understanding of scripture must be exposed to the full range of literary experience.'[18] This, I think, would only be a gesture in the present circumstances. Nevertheless, it is not difficult to imagine a certain kind of reaction to our problem which would see this gesture, and others like it, as irrelevant as a religious response. They would probably tell us to stop worrying about the *language*. Concentrate on the heart of religion—*live* the religious life, *re-enact* the deeds of Jesus, and so on; the *language* will look after itself. Unfortunately, the matter is not as simple as this tempting reaction implies. In so far as a believer utters words about what he does, his *way* of talking is inseparable from *what* he talks about. To use Ian Robinson's literary terms, a failure in style is not a *separate* failure. Someone *could* read the N.E.B. and see Jesus as some kind of Victorian governess. Anyone who has attempted to study the N.E.B. with a class of fifteen-year-olds would probably confirm this. It is simply not the case that *any* report of the deeds of Jesus would allow his actions to *speak for themselves.*

[17] *Literature and Dogma*, p. 47.
[18] *The Prose For God*, p. 44.

Even at the sophisticated level of the modern theologian's attempt to reinterpret Christianity, what appear to be transparently attractive options to the theologian may fail to be evocative in the desired way in the minds of his readers. Alistair Kee, in a similar way to Arnold's use of the term 'Eternal', suggests the phrase, 'the way of transcendence', as an alternative to the more traditional words which expressed the sense of the reality of God for the Hebrews and early Christians.[19] Monica Furlong finds Kee's interpretation, with its 'challenges' and 'decisions', as having 'a muscular ring reminiscent of *Scouting for Boys*'.[20] She comments that the word 'God' would probably be *more* evocative than 'the way of transcendence' in non-academic and non-theological circles. I am not concerned to argue the case here. I simply record this reaction to Kee's language. Some people may see Jesus as a Victorian governess in the N.E.B. and as the Chief Scout in Kee's analysis. They are not necessarily choosing the 'way of immanence' and rejecting the 'way of transcendence'. The *way* of talking has not been strong enough to bear *what* is being talked about.

When the Wittgensteinians talk about the possibility of 'pictures' dying, they mean that the possibilities for meaning which they carried may disappear from the language. The *language* they refer to is the *first order* language of believers with its complex relation to language and culture in general. It is not possible for the theologian to hold on heroically to these possibilities of meaning in his *second order* explication of beliefs. As Phillips comments,[21] a theologian is not someone who knows more about God than anyone else; he is someone who makes clear the 'grammar' of religious belief. This does not mean that he is engaged in a solely 'bookish' activity. The 'grammar' of belief has to do with the totality of the religious life. It is not he, for example, who decides

[19] See esp. the last four chapters of *The Way of Transcendence*.
[20] *The End of Our Exploring* (Hodder, London, 1973), p. 165.
[21] Review of *The Edges of Language* (P. van Buren), *Theology*, March 1973 Vol. LXXVI No. 633, pp. 152–3.

that we need a *new theology*, or, in Wittgensteinian terms, a *reformed grammar*. Where there is a genuine demand for a new theology, it does not emerge in a vacuum from the theoretical and arbitrary insistence of a few theologians. A genuine demand arises from the totality of the religious life in its desire to say something fresh to God and about God.[22] If this is true, it may explain the air of artificiality and the sense of hopelessness which pervades many works of modern theology—even the apparently most confident kind. They are often attempts to reinstate at a second-order level what is not there at the first-order level, i.e., in what believers actually do, think and say. Thus, Langdon Gilkey's *Naming the Whirlwind: The Renewal of God-Language*[23] tries to show that the religious dimension of ultimacy is, in fact, a *presupposition* of secular life and language. Religious discourse becomes essential, he claims, when we encounter the 'limits' of our secular categories. Even though people may not use first-order religious language, their most serious concerns are apparently ready for 'baptism' by the discerning theologian: 'Religious discourse is essential if secular life is to achieve a creative worldliness.'[24] Creating religious beliefs 'by definition' is the besetting temptation for the theologian in a period when religious discourse appears to be absent. It is hard for the theologian to accept that the very stuff of his trade may 'become obsolete and get forgotten'.

The problems are very different, of course, for those who maintain—against the Wittgensteinian view—that 'God' is a *name* for some kind of fact. It may be worthwhile glancing at this alternative approach.

The Facts Beyond the Language

Theologians and philosophers who argue that God is in some sense a 'fact' are bound to see the present dilemma for

[22] See *Athronyddu am Grefydd*, p. 40.
[23] (Bobbs-Merrill, New York, 1969).
[24] Ibid., p. 364.

religious belief in very different terms. 'God', in this sense, is *there* whether human beings believe in Him or not. His reality does not depend upon human concepts and language. Man's *consciousness* of His reality may be greatly affected by the state of a culture and a language, but this is a different matter.

People who say that religious language has a factual grammar do not, of course, mean that *every* religious utterance *refers to* something. Hick, like many others, argues that much religious language is mythological, poetic and emotive.[25] He has recently argued, for example, that the language of the Incarnation is mythological.[26] Such myths, however, derive their religious significance, and are saved from being merely arbitrary constructions of the imagination because they are set within 'a framework of factual belief which they supplement and adorn.'[27] Since I have mentioned Hick's work, it may be useful to see what the logic of the 'fact-stating' position amounts to. Whatever we may say about the adequacy of Hick's overall position, he has stated the *logic* of it in a very clear way.[28]

For Hick, the final point of distinction between religion, on the one hand, and aesthetics and ethics, on the other, is the *ontological* claim that God exists as a real Being.[29] The problem which Hick often calls the 'cognitive—noncognitive issue' is one which centres upon the 'metaphysical surplus', namely, the reference to God. He acknowledges the possibility, in principle, of forming a coherent understanding of the universe without reference to God, i.e., the sheer givenness of the universe is accepted as the 'ultimate fact'.[30] By contrast, for the theist, the 'ultimate fact' is God.

---

[25] *God and the Universe of Faiths*, p. vii.
[26] Ibid., p. 165.
[27] Ibid., pp. 23f.
[28] For a general criticism of Hick's work see J. H. Gill, 'John Hick and Religious Knowledge' *International Journal for Philosophy of Religion*, Fall 1971 Vol. 2 No. 3, pp. 129–47.
[29] J. Hick, *Faith and Knowledge* (Macmillan, London, 1967 2nd edn.), p. 145.
[30] *God and the Universe of Faiths*, p. 94.

From this point of view, 'what there is' or 'how things are'[31] is only rightly understood by reference to God.

Hick sometimes distinguishes between the ways of accepting either the universe or God as 'ultimate' by claiming that the Christian believes in the existence of 'religious facts'.[32] A transcendent order of fact 'sustains and governs all the more proximate types of fact'.[33] Nevertheless, if claims about religious facts are to avoid emptiness they cannot be immune from questions about grounds, meaning and verification.[34] According to Hick, the core of the concept of verification is 'the removal of ignorance or uncertainty concerning the truth of a proposition'.[35] If anything is described as factual, whether it be a 'religious' fact or a 'more proximate' kind of fact, it must make an experienceable difference whether or not such facts exist.[36] Hick claims that there is, in fact, a fundamental element of Christian belief which meets the demand for an experienceable difference and also for the removal of uncertainty about its truth, namely, the eschatological element. For Hick, this notion is indispensable for any conception of the universe which claims to be Christian.[37] That is, the Christian concept of God has, as a corollary, eschatological expectations which will be ultimately fulfilled or not fulfilled.[38] Hick's concept of 'eschatological verification' is, of course, intended to establish th : cognitive *meaningfulness* and not the truth of religious belief. Nevertheless, it does not follow from all this that religious belief is an explanatory hypothesis for Hick: 'I regard it

[31] Ibid., p. vii.
[32] *Faith and Knowledge*, p. 193.
[33] *Faith and the Philosophers* ed. J. Hick (Macmillan, London, 1964), p. 239.
[34] Ibid., p. 241.
[35] *Faith and Knowledge*, p. 169.
[36] See *Philosophy of Religion*, p. 96 and *Faith and Knowledge*, pp. 166f.
[37] *Faith and the Philosophers*, p. 249.
[38] *Faith and Knowledge*, p. 197. Eschatological verification has been widely discussed, e.g., K. Nielsen, 'Eschatological Verification' *Canadian Journal of Theology*, 1963 Vol. IX No. 4, pp. 271–81; W. Bean, 'Eschatological Verification . . . Fortress or Fairyland?' *Methodos*, 1964, XVI, pp. 91–107.

rather as consciousness of God and as living on the basis of that consciousness.'[39]

Hick's views represent a straightforward example of the *logic* of the fact-stating position. It does not underlie *all* the accounts which see God's existence as a *sort of fact*. Different metaphysical systems, whether they be in terms of Being, Process, and so on, will fill out the fact-stating case in many different ways. However it is defined, 'God' will be some kind of 'metaphysical fact' in these various systems. 'God' will have a referent.

The late Ian T. Ramsey was a philosopher who attempted to interpret religious language in a way which preserved its 'objective reference'. There is no space here for a full account of his position,[40] but a few references to his works may illuminate the alternative I am considering. Ramsey argued that to understand the *true grammar* of religious language we must look to the rock from which it is hewn, namely, a cosmic disclosure. 'Disclosures' must be understood in the sense of situations 'coming alive', 'taking on depth', etc. A *cosmic* disclosure is one which reveals something of universal significance;[41] it has an absolute character;[42] it is all inclusive.[43] To make intellectual sense of our talk of disclosures, Ramsey believes that we need metaphysics to provide an ancillary scheme[44] in order to plot our 'cosmic position'.[45] We want to know how our fragmentary disclosures relate to the universe in general. Metaphysics, for

---

[39] *God and the Universe of Faiths*, p. 32.
[40] See D. Evans, 'Ian Ramsey on Talk About God' *Religious Studies* Vol. 7, 1971, pp. 125–40, 213–26; J. H. Gill 'The Language of Theology: Martin Heidegger or Ian Ramsey?' *Encounter*, Summer 1967 XXXVII, pp. 195–225.
[41] I. T. Ramsey, *Christian Discourse* (O.U.P., London, 1965), p. 7.
[42] *Models for Divine Activity*, p. 60.
[43] I. T. Ramsey, 'Reply to Critics' *Theoria to Theory*, April 1967 Vol. 1, p. 265.
[44] I. T. Ramsey, 'On the Possibility and Purpose of a Metaphysical Theology' in I. T. Ramsey (ed.), *Prospect for Metaphysics* (Allen & Unwin, London, 1961), p. 157.
[45] Ibid., p. 153.

Ramsey, is not merely an ancillary map: 'it is . . . the construction of a map in accordance with a vision of the unseen.'[46] Ramsey's paradigm case of the 'unseen' which gives him the confidence to pursue such a vision is that of the 'I' which is *more* than the observables.[47]

Ramsey's own 'vision' is, of course, *theistic*. For him, 'God' is the 'integrator word' which provides—in contrast to other words, 'I', 'Being', 'Absolute', etc.,—the most 'simple, far-reaching and coherent metaphysical map'.[48] Ramsey claims that 'we are entitled to speak of there being a single individuation expressing itself in each and all of these disclosures'.[49] To do justice to the range and subtlety of Ramsey's thought we should need to peg back the few things said here on to a much wider treatment, such as that suggested by the title of a book which Ramsey promised to write but did not live to produce, namely, *Fact, Metaphysics and God*.[50]

By glancing at Ramsey's work it is possible to see how grave problems may face even the 'fact-stating' view in a particular culture. Ramsey often remarked that he was attempting to *broaden* contemporary empiricism. His way of doing so was to argue for the *empirical possibility* of disclosures; the crucial issue, as he saw it, 'between the 'believing' and the 'unbelieving' empiricist today'.[51] Ramsey resists any view which reduces all experience to sense-experience. Our experience amounts to *more* than that of isolated phenomena impressing themselves upon us. The whole is *more* than the sum of its parts, and so on. 'Sensate' is perhaps an apt word to describe the 'unbelieving'

46 Ibid., p. 163.
47 Ibid., p. 163, and see *Christian Empiricism*, pp. 62f.
48 *Prospect for Metaphysics*, p. 164.
49 'Talk About God' in I. T. Ramsey (ed.) *Words About God* (S.C.M., London, 1971), p. 212.
50 See *Religious Language* (S.C.M., London, 1967 edn.), p. 9, *Christian Empiricism* p. 239, and the comment in D. L. Edwards, *Ian Ramsey; Bishop of Durham—A Memoir* (O.U.P., London, 1973), p. 60.
51 *Christian Empiricism*, p. 15, n. 20.

empiricist in Ramsey's arguments. Peter Berger quotes Kahn's and Wiener's description of the projected course of twentieth century cultures: ' "... empirical, this-worldly, secular, humanistic, pragmatic, utilitarian, contractual, epicurean or hedonistic . . ." '[52] Such a world would be uncongenial for Ramsey's disclosures. His analyses are a standing protest against such a grim prospect. Yet, even if Ramsey is right about disclosures in the most general sense, this does not, of course, *guarantee* the religious position. It simply means that there is a currency in ordinary use which Ramsey thinks is 'apt' for the religious use.

There is therefore an element of fatality in both the Wittgensteinian and some versions of the 'fact-stating' view. Religious belief on the Wittgensteinian view depends upon the *possibility* of an *expressive language* in the culture. The other standpoint—as it is represented by Ramsey at least—depends upon the *empirical possibility of disclosures*. Nevertheless, there is a crucial difference between the two positions. On the 'fact-stating' view God would exist in some sense *independently* of the sensitivities of man. God would be in eclipse at a time when men did not believe.

Two Standpoints in Tension—a Dispute about Foundations

To draw a crude distinction between the Wittgensteinian and the 'fact-stating' approaches, we can again use Hick's terminology. For the Wittgensteinians, the world is the 'ultimate fact'. On the opposite view, only *God* can be the 'ultimate fact'. The terms of the distinction as I have drawn it here would hardly satisfy the Wittgensteinians. It will do, however, as a way-in to people who may be unfamiliar with this way of looking at the problem. Let me expand on the distinction.

The sociologist, Peter Berger, has several strong things to say[53] about the way secular theologians accommodate

[52] *A Rumour of Angels* (Penguin Books, 1971), p. 13.
[53] 'A Sociological View of the Secularization of Theology' *Journal for the Scientific Study of Religion*, Vol. VI No. 1, Spring 1967, pp. 3–16.

themselves to the critical canons of secular society. 'The fundamental religious proposition,' says Berger, '. . . is that man is not alone in reality.'[54] For him there is a straight choice; 'Is man alone in reality: yes or no? If one is certain that the answer is "Yes", then, it seems to me, one could do better things with one's time than theology.'[55] For Berger this is the knot in the thread; it is the essence of the matter. It is reminiscent of the philosopher Williams' test to see whether it is Christianity which is being discussed in any particular case.[56] It would not be difficult to show that many theologians also make this kind of stipulation of the irreducible core of religious belief. John Macquarrie, for example, insists upon the centrality of the problem of God in spite of the prevalent fashions of the theologies *of* (hope, play, revolution, etc.); 'For unless reality is trustworthy at the deepest level (and this, I take it, is the *fundamental meaning* of belief in God) there is little ground for hope, and celebration becomes irrelevant.'[57] The Process theologian, Schubert Ogden, makes a similar point: 'the *primary use* or function of "God" is to refer to the objective ground in reality itself of our ineradicable confidence in the final worth of our existence.'[58] However difficult the foundation may be to define, a foundation it seems is what there must be for most theologians.

This kind of stipulation is not confined to the more overtly metaphysical theologians. Kee's *The Way of Transcendence* has all the trappings of radicalism ('Christian Faith without Belief in God' as a sub-title, etc.), but even he admits that we are faced unavoidably with the 'mysterious and awesome question': '. . . what kind of reality is it which invites faith in transcendence and then *confirms* that faith?'[59] Kee

---

54 Ibid., p. 16.
55 Ibid., p. 16.
56 See above p. 122.
57 *Thinking About God* (S.C.M., London, 1975), p. 87; my italics.
58 *The Reality of God* (S.C.M., London, 1967), p. 37; my italics.
59 *The Way of Transcendence*, p. 231; my italics.

comes to this admission rather late in his book and a foot-
note on the final page admits that there must be 'ontological
implications' for choosing the way of transcendence,
although we are apparently not in a position to formulate
a 'satisfactory ontology' at the present time.[60] Kee's
radicalism does not extend to questioning whether *any*
ontology is necessary. By asking about the reality which
confirms faith in transcendence, is he not giving *theoretical*
content to religious beliefs just as much as the metaphysical
theologies he criticizes? That is to say, is he not looking for
something *outside* the belief to confirm it?

The question that arises is whether the assertion that there
must be a *foundation* to belief (or something outside of it
which confirms it) cuts across the very essence of religion.
The Wittgensteinians have developed a definition of genuine
religion which strongly rejects any element of 'confirmation' or compensation and consolation for that matter. The
world is given and religion is a way of responding to contingency. This position, by definition, is not interested in
'more facts' of any kind, or a reality which *confirms* it. The
religious view must be religious from the start. It does not
depend on *any* foundation. Nevertheless, there is something
about the Wittgensteinian view which makes it more difficult to accept than the alternative I have discussed. Hick, for
example, regards the Wittgensteinian view as 'a spiritually
elitist view which disregards the large and very imperfect
mass of humanity'.[61] The future is bleak for the millions
today who have little prospect of human fulfilment if there
is no transcendent order of fact. This 'reminder' from the
'fact-stating' side is not likely, however, to carry much
weight for the Wittgensteinians; they begin with an idea of
religion which has to assume this sad feature of human life.
There is a tendency in many of us to feel that there *must* be
something substantive which religious language refers to if

[60]   *The Way of Transcendence*, p. 234.
[61]   *God and the Universe of Faiths*, p. 35.

religion is to be religion. Paul Tillich recalls[62] that the philo-sophy of values dominated all the important theological faculties when he began his theological studies in 1904. With his fellow students he revolted against this for both theoretical and emotional reasons: 'We did not accept the defeat of metaphysics and the flight into the defenses of the value theory as final. *We wanted being.*'[63] We could say that Tillich's feelings are very strong here precisely because, as Wittgenstein claimed, the tendencies to give a foundation to our language run very deep. In his sermons and addresses to the lay mind, Tillich spoke about religion as 'ultimate concern' which is quite close to the Wittgensteinian stress on the all-regulating character of the religious 'picture'. However, when he addressed himself to intellectuals, Tillich quite clearly insisted on the need to ground religious values in 'Being'.[64] At this point, of course, Tillich and Wittgen-stein go their separate ways.

There is no easy way of resolving the differences between the two views I have been discussing. As I suggested earlier, it is perhaps best not to regard either view as a reductionist version of the other's estimate of what religion essentially is. Both alternatives are radically different ways of seeing religious belief. To summarize the state of the debate in a very general way, we could say that the onus is on the fact-stating view to develop an acceptable metaphysical frame-work, and that the onus is on the Wittgensteinians to offer an analysis of religion which is no less profound in the absence of a substantive reference for religious language.[65]

---

[62] 'Is a Science of Human Values Possible?' in A. H. Maslow (ed.), *New Knowledge in Human Values* (Harper & Row, New York, 1959), pp. 189–196.

[63] Ibid., p. 191.

[64] See A. C. MacIntyre's comments (with P. Ricoeur) in *The Religious Significance of Atheism* (Columbia Univ. Press, New York, 1969), p. 27.

[65] I have argued elsewhere that John Wisdom appears to use the language of both alternatives, but that in the last analysis he too takes the Wittgen-steinian road; see *The Grammar of God*, unpublished dissertation Ph.D., Birmingham University 1974, esp. Chap. 5.

Conclusion

I HAVE suggested that in the work of Wittgenstein and his
followers there is implicit a view of religion which could
say a great deal to our modern religious traditions. The
reason for saying this is not because it is 'relevant' to contemporary theologies and religious sensibilities. Wittgenstein's memory should not be desecrated by making him a
posthumous contributor to passing theological fashions. We
need to pay attention to Wittgenstein's work because it is
intrinsically important. However, I have referred to contemporary theology in order to gain some bearings for
locating Wittgenstein in the midst of the many competing
philosophical and theological voices. In modern jargon,
Wittgenstein's thought on religious belief combines a very
radical treatment of metaphysics with a conservative view of
religious language.

If Wittgenstein's work had seriously influenced modern
theologians, there would have been a radical change of
direction in their deliberations. There would have been a
move away from the concern to interpret the faith through
either modern speculative philosophies or the secular *Zeit-
geist*, towards a search for a genuinely expressive religious
language—a 'prose for God'. The latter would, of course,
be a *search* rather than an *invention*. But would this not be to
canonize Wittgenstein as a philosophical saint in the same
tradition as Whitehead, Heidegger, etc.? I think not.
Wittgenstein offers us no *theories*. He puts philosophy forward as an *activity* to ease our mental cramps.

Wittgenstein's name has probably suffered in theological
colleges and similar circles through its association with van

Buren's *The Secular Meaning of the Gospel*.[1] There is irony in this. The whole idea of a *secular* meaning for religion seems foreign to Wittgenstein. Even where Wittgenstein's name is not linked with hostile scepticism, he suffers by association with a form of religious reductionism. I hope that this study has shown that Wittgenstein's work raises the whole question of just what reductionism is in religion. In a way, Wittgenstein's ideas are more lethal than the straightforward empiricism of Ayer, Flew, etc., because they imply a view of religion which indirectly claims to be more *religious* than many of the current conceptions.

The question that the Wittgensteinian approach puts relentlessly to philosophical theology is just what stake Christianity has in metaphysics. What exactly is *reduced* or *lost* by ceasing to connect religious language to something external? This is a very difficult question to answer. It depends upon what one judges religious belief to be, and there is a very complex relation between the beliefs themselves and the philosophical accounts of them. Granted this complex relation, does Wittgenstein's influence extend beyond philosophy to the religious life itself? Is there the seed for a new Christianity in the Wittgensteinian view? No doubt the Wittgensteinians themselves would feel uneasy with this question. After all, their whole point is to claim that they are bringing out something which has been there all along; the distinction between the temporal and the eternal, etc. However, someone could be forgiven for thinking that the religion underlying the Wittgensteinian analyses is something new. Flew draws attention to the difference between Phillips' view of religious belief and that of most believers and observes that Phillips could say 'that he has outlined a religion which is his own, and superior to most of the competition. This would, I believe, be true'.[2] It would need a full-scale study to demonstrate it, but at first glance

[1] (S.C.M., London, 1963).
[2] *Philosophical Books*, May 1971 Vol. XII No. 2, pp. 23–4.

there is much in the writings of St John of the Cross, Kierkegaard, Tolstoy, Simone Weil and Thomas Merton which is compatible with Phillips' work. If the Wittgensteinian writings do point to the seed of a new Christianity, it was probably a seed already sown in the work of this tradition of thinkers.

The Wittgensteinian conception of what genuine religion amounts to means that they do not claim to give an account of the entire range of belief and commitment we find that believers actually have. However, as the Wittgensteinians would probably say themselves, the language of the kind of religion they admire is in decline. To admit this is to give oneself a feeling of powerlessness—some language-games become obsolete and get forgotten. They may not be 'forgotten' by a minority of individuals, but such a group could hardly hope to stage-manage a culture. Religious language is 'consecrated by use' but it may prove more and more difficult to go on using it with the same sense. To use the language of the early Wittgenstein, the meaning of the language of religion may cease to *show itself*. Paul Engelmann, Wittgenstein's friend in the early years, believed, as we have seen, that Wittgenstein's language was best thought of as the language of 'wordless faith'.[3] Engelmann thought that if the *new spiritual attitude* he saw embodied in Wittgenstein was expressed in the deeds of other people, there would be no need to *describe* this attitude in words.[4] I drew attention earlier in this study to the radicality of Engelmann's scepticism about language: '. . . any doctrine uttered in words is the source of its own misconstruction by worshippers, disciples and supporters.'[5] There are obviously very great difficulties in recommending Engelmann's idea of 'wordless faith' to believers who want to survive the decline of an expressive language. Yet, if there ever is a time when the

---

[3] *Letters from Ludwig Wittgenstein with a Memoir*, p. 135.
[4] Ibid., pp. 135–6.
[5] Ibid., p. 136.

language of religion fails to 'speak', the believer is bound to hope that his actions will 'speak louder' than the language which now distorts his beliefs to the minds of his unbelieving contemporaries. In such a time, there is a sense in which the believer's faith will have to be 'wordless'.

Bibliography

Anscombe, G. E. M., 'Misinformation: What Wittgenstein Really Said', *The Tablet*, 17th April 1954, p. 373.

Arnold, Matthew, *Literature and Dogma* (Smith, Elder, London, 1900.)

God and the Bible (Smith, Elder, London, 1889).

Barbour, Ian G., *Myths, Models and Paradigms* (S.C.M., London, 1974).

Bartley, William Warren, *Wittgenstein* (Quartet, London, 1974).

Bean, William, 'Eschatological Verification . . . Fortress or Fairyland?' *Methodos*, 1964 XVI, pp. 91–107.

Bell, Richard Henry, *Theology as Grammar* (unpublished dissertation), Yale University Ph.D. 1968.

'Wittgenstein and Descriptive Theology', *Religious Studies*, Oct. 1969, Vol. 5 No. 1, pp. 1–18.

Berger, Peter L., *A Rumour of Angels* (Penguin, Harmondsworth, 1971).

'A Sociological View of the Secularization of Theology' *Journal for the Scientific Study of Religion*, Vol. VI No. 1, Spring 1967, pp. 3–16.

Bonhoeffer, Dietrich. *Letters and Papers from Prison* (Fontana, London, 1965).

Bouwsma, O. K., 'Anselm's Argument', *The Nature of Philosophical Enquiry*, ed. Joseph Bobik (University of Notre Dame 1970).

Braithwaite, R. B., 'An Empiricist's View of the Nature of Religious Belief', *The Philosophy of Religion*, ed. B. Mitchell (O.U.P. 1971).

Camus, Albert, *The Myth of Sisyphus* (Vintage, New York, 1955).

Selected Essays and Notebooks (Penguin, Harmondsworth, 1970).

Carnap, Rudolf, 'Autobiography', *The Philosophy of Carnap*, ed. P. Schlipp (Open Court, Illinois, 1964).

Dilman, Ilham, *Induction and Deduction* (Blackwell, Oxford, 1973).

'Wittgenstein on the Soul' in The Royal Institute of Philosophy

Lectures, Vol. 7 1972–73, *Understanding Wittgenstein* (Macmillan, London, 1974), pp. 162–92.

Durrant, Michael, *The Logical Status of 'God'* (Macmillan, London, 1973).

Edwards, David L., Ian Ramsey, Bishop of Durham: A Memoir (O.U.P., London, 1973).

Engelmann, Paul, *Letters from Ludwig Wittgenstein with a Memoir* (Blackwell, Oxford, 1967).

Evans, Donald, 'Ian Ramsey on Talk About God', *Religious Studies* 7 Part 1: pp. 125–40; Part 2: pp. 213–26.

Fann, K. T., *Wittgenstein's Conception of Philosophy* (Blackwell, Oxford, 1969).

Flew, Antony, 'Anthropology and Rationality', *Question* No. 5 1972.

'Conversations with the Master', *Spectator*, 16th Sept. 1966, p. 355.

Review of *Death and Immortality* (D. Z. Phillips) *Philosophical Books*, May 1971 Vol. XII No. 2, pp. 23–4.

Furlong, Monica, *The End of Our Exploring* (Hodder and Stoughton, London 1973).

Gellner, Ernest, *Cause and Meaning in the Social Sciences* (Routledge and Kegan Paul, London, 1973).

Gilkey, Langdon, *Naming the Whirlwind: The Renewal of God-Language* (Bobbs-Merrill, New York, 1969).

Gill, Jerry H., 'The Language of Theology: Martin Heidegger or Ian Ramsey?', *Encounter*, Summer 1967 XXXVII, pp. 195–225.

'John Hick and Religious Knowledge', *International Journal for Philosophy of Religion*, Fall 1971 Vol. 2 No. 3, pp. 129–47.

Gregor, I. and Stein, W. (eds.), *The Prose For God* (Sheed & Ward, London, 1973).

Hepburn, R. W., Review of *The Concept of Prayer* (D. Z. Phillips) *Philosophical Books*, May 1966 Vol. VII No. 2, pp. 23–5.

Hick, John, *Faith and Knowledge* (Macmillan, London, 1967 2nd edn).

Philosophy of Religion (Prentice Hall, New Jersey, 1973 2nd edn).

God and the Universe of Faiths (Macmillan, London, 1973).

'Sceptics and Believers', *Faith and the Philosophers* ed. John Hick (Macmillan, London, 1964).

Review of *Do Religious Claims Make Sense?* (S. C. Brown) *Philosophical Books,* May 1970 Vol. XI No. 2, pp. 3–4.

High, Dallas M., *Language, Persons and Belief* (O.U.P., New York, 1967).

'Belief, Falsification and Wittgenstein', *International Journal for Philosophy of Religion,* Winter 1972 Vol. 3 No. 4, pp. 240–50.

Holmer, Paul L., 'Wittgenstein and Theology', *New Essays in Religious Language,* ed. Dallas M. High (O.U.P., New York, 1969), pp. 25–35.

Hordern, William, *Speaking of God* (Epworth, London, 1965).

Hudson, W. Donald, *Ludwig Wittgenstein* (Lutterworth, London, 1968).

A Philosophical Approach to Religion (Macmillan, London, 1974).

'Some Remarks on Wittgenstein's Account of Religious Belief', G. Vesey, et. al., *Talk of God* (Macmillan, London, 1969), pp. 36–51.

'On Two points Against Wittgensteinian Fideism', *Philosophy,* 43 1968, pp. 269–73.

' "Using a Picture" and Religious Belief', *Sophia,* July 1973 Vol. XII No. 2, pp. 11–17.

Hunter, J. F. M., ' "Forms of Life" in Wittgenstein's Philosophical Investigations', *American Philosophical Quarterly,* Oct. 1968 Vol. 5, pp. 233–43.

Irving, John A., 'Mysticism and the Limits of Communication', *Mysticism and the Modern Mind,* ed. A. P. Stiernotte (Liberal Arts, New York, 1959).

Janik, Allan and Toulmin, Stephen, *Wittgenstein's Vienna* (Weidenfeld & Nicolson, London, 1973).

Jones, J. R., 'Gwirionedd ac Ystyr', *Saith Ysgrif ar Grefydd,* ed. D. Z. Phillips (Gee Press 1967), pp. 51–68.

'Ontoleg Ffydd', *Diwinyddiaeth* XX 1969, pp. 19–34.

'Love as Perception of Meaning', *Religion and Understanding* ed. D. Z. Phillips (Blackwell, Oxford, 1967), pp. 141–53.

Kasachkoff, Tziporah, 'Talk about God's Existence', *Philosophical Studies* (The National University of Ireland) 1970 Vol. XIX, pp. 181–92.

Kee, Alistair, *The Way of Transcendence* (Penguin, Harmondsworth, 1971).

Keightley, Alan, *The Grammar of God*, unpublished Ph.D. dissertation, Birmingham University, 1974.

Kierkegaard, Soren, *Purity of Heart* (Fontana, London, 1961).

King-Farlow, John and Christensen, William H, *Faith and The Life of Reason* (D. Reidel, Holland, 1972).

Kuhn, Thomas S., *The Structure of Scientific Revolutions* (University of Chicago, 1973, 2nd edn).

Ladd, John (ed.), *Ethical Relativism* (Wadsworth, California, 1973).

Lakatos, I. and Musgrove, A., *Criticism and the Growth of Knowledge* (C.U.P., Cambridge, 1970).

McGuinness, B. F. M., 'The Mysticism of the *Tractatus*', *Philosophical Review* 1966 Vol. 75, pp. 305–28.

MacIntyre, A. C., *The Religious Significance of Atheism* (with P. Ricoeur) (Columbia University, New York, 1969).

Macquarrie, John, *Thinking About God* (S.C.M., London, 1975).

Magee, Bryan, *Modern British Philosophy* (Paladin, London, 1973).

Malcolm, Norman, *Ludwig Wittgenstein: A Memoir*, with a Biographical Sketch by George H. von Wright (O.U.P., London, 1966).

'Wittgenstein's Philosophical Investigations' in G. Pitcher (ed.) *Wittgenstein: The Philosophical Investigations* (Macmillan, London, 1970 edn).

Meynell, Hugo, 'Truth, Witchcraft and Professor Winch', *The Heythrop Journal*, May 1972, pp. 162–73.

'Kai Nielsen and the Concept of God', *Question* 5 1972, pp. 48–54.

Miles, T. R., *Religion and the Scientific Outlook* (Allen & Unwin, London, 1959).

Mitchell, Basil, *The Justification of Religious Belief* (Macmillan, London, 1973).

Moore, G. E., 'Wittgenstein's Lectures in 1930–33', *Mind* Part 1: 1954 Vol. 63, pp. 1–15; Part 2: 1954 Vol. 63, pp. 289–315; Part 3: 1955 Vol. 64, pp. 1–27.

Philosophical Papers (Allen & Unwin, London, 1959).

Mounce, H. O., 'Understanding a Primitive Society', *Philosophy*, Oct., 1973 Vol. 48, pp. 347–62.

Mundle, C. W. K., *A Critique of Linguistic Philosophy* (Clarendon, Oxford, 1970).

Munitz, M. K., *The Mystery of Existence* (Appleton-Century-Crofts, New York, 1965).

Nielsen, Kai, *Contemporary Critiques of Religion* (Macmillan, London, 1971).

Scepticism (Macmillan, London, 1973).

'Wittgensteinian Fideism Again: A Reply to Hudson', *Philosophy*, Vol. XLIV 1969, pp. 63–5.

'Eschatological Verification', *Canadian Journal of Theology*, 1963 Vol. IX No. 4, pp. 271–81.

'A Reply to Hugo Meynell', *Question* 5 1972, pp. 55–62.

Nietzsche, F., *My Sister and I* (Bridgehead Books, New York, 1965).

Ogden, S., *The Reality of God* (S.C.M., London, 1967).

Onimus, Jean, *Albert Camus and Christianity* (Gill & Macmillan, Dublin, 1970).

Palmer, H., 'Understanding First', *Theology*, March 1968 Vol. LXXI No. 573, pp. 107–14.

Phillips, Dewi Z., *The Concept of Prayer* (Routledge and Kegan Paul, London, 1965).

Faith and Philosophical Enquiry (Routledge and Kegan Paul, London, 1970).

Death and Immortality (Macmillan, London, 1970).

Athronyddu am Grefydd: Cyfeiriadau Newydd (Gomer Press, 1974).

Some Limits to Moral Endeavour (Inaugural Lecture) University College of Swansea 1971.

(ed.) *Religion and Understanding* (Blackwell, Oxford, 1967).

(ed.) *Saith Ysgrif ar Grefydd* (Gee Press 1967).

'Moral Presuppositions and Literary Criticism', *The Human World*, Feb. 1972 No. 6, pp. 24–34.

'Allegiance and Change in Morality: A Study in Contrasts', *Philosophy and the Arts* (Royal Institute of Philosophy Lectures, Vol. 6 1971–2) (Macmillan, London, 1973), pp. 47–64.

'Introduction' in J. L. Stocks *Morality and Purpose* (Routledge and Kegan Paul, London, 1969), pp. 1–14.

'Y Syniad o Fywyd Tragwyddol', *Y Dysgedydd*, Jan.–Feb. 1961, pp. 15–20.

'Credu neu Beidio—pa Wahaniaeth?' *Barn*, July 1964, pp. 250–251.

'Angau a Tragwyddoldeb', *Saith Ysgrif ar Grefydd* ed. D. Z. Phillips (Gee Press), pp. 119–38.

'Credu ac Anghredu', *Diwinyddiaeth*, 1968 No. XIX, pp. 11–19.

'Gwirionedd, Ystyr, a Chrefydd', *Diwinyddiaeth* No XX, pp. 3–18.

Review of *The Edges of Language* (by Paul van Buren), *Theology*, March 1973 Vol. LXXVI No. 633, pp. 152–3.

and Mounce, H. O., *Moral Practices* (Routledge and Kegan Paul, London, 1969).

and Dilman, I., *Sense and Delusion* (Routledge and Kegan Paul, London, 1971).

Pitkin, Hanna F., *Wittgenstein and Justice* (University of California 1972).

Plato, *Gorgias* (Penguin 1973 edn).

Ramsey, Ian T., *Christian Discourse* (O.U.P., London, 1965).

Religious Language (S.C.M., London, 1957 edn).

Models for Divine Activity (S.C.M., London, 1973).

Christian Empiricism (ed. Jerry H. Gill) (Sheldon, London, 1974).

'On the Possibility and Purpose of a Metaphysical Theology', *Prospect for Metaphysics* ed. I. T. Ramsey (Allen & Unwin, London, 1961), pp. 153–77.

(ed.) *Words About God* (S.C.M., London, 1971).

'Reply to Critics', *Theoria to Theory*, April 1967 Vol. 1 3rd quarter, pp. 263–9.

Rhees, Rush, *Without Answers* (Routledge and Kegan Paul, London, 1969).

Discussions of Wittgenstein (Routledge and Kegan Paul, London, 1970).

'Could language be invented by a Robinson Crusoe?' *The Private Language Argument* ed. O. R. Jones. (Macmillan, London, 1971), pp. 61–75.

'Introduction'—'Wittgenstein's Remarks on Frazer's "Golden Bough" ', *The Human World*, May 1971 No. 3, pp. 18–28.

Robinson, Ian, *The Survival of English* (C.U.P., Cambridge, 1973).

Robinson, John A. T., 'Has "God" a Meaning?', *Question*, 1 Feb. 1968, pp. 55–61.

Roszak, Theodore, *Where the Wasteland Ends* (Faber & Faber, London, 1973).

Rudich, N. and Stassen, M., 'Wittgenstein's Implied Anthropology: Remarks on Wittgenstein's Notes on Frazer', *History and Theory*, Vol. 10 1971, pp. 84–9.

Russell, Bertrand, *The Autobiography of Bertrand Russell* (Allen & Unwin, London, 1975 edn).

Sherry, Patrick J., *Truth and the 'Religious Language Game'* unpublished Ph.D. dissertation, Cambridge University, 1971.

   'Is Religion a "Form of Life"?', *American Philosophical Quarterly*, April 1972 Vol. 9 No. 2, pp. 159–67.

   'Learning how to be Religious' (The Work of Paul Holmer,) *Theology*, Feb. 1974, pp. 81–90.

Smart, Ninian, *The Science of Religion and the Sociology of Knowledge* (Princeton University 1973).

   The Religious Experience of Mankind (Fontana, London, 1971).

Sprague, Elmer, 'On Professor Tillich's Ontological Question', *International Philosophical Quarterly*, 1962 No. 2, pp. 81–91.

Stocks, J. L., *Morality and Purpose* (Routledge and Kegan Paul, London, 1969).

Sutherland, S. R., 'Religion and Ethics', *The Human World*, Nov. 1971 No. 5, pp. 40–52.

Tillich, Paul, 'Is A Science of Human Values Possible?', *New Knowledge in Human Values*, ed. A. H. Maslow (Harper, New York, 1959), pp. 189–96.

Trigg, Roger, *Reason and Commitment* (C.U.P., Cambridge, 1973).

Unamuno, Miguel de, *The Tragic Sense of Life* (Fontana, London, 1962 edn).

van Buren, Paul, *The Secular Meaning of the Gospel* (S.C.M., London, 1963).

   Theological Explorations (S.C.M., London, 1968).

   The Edges of Language (S.C.M., London, 1972).

Waismann, F., *Ludwig Wittgenstein und der Wiener Kreis* (ed. B. F. McGuinness) (Blackwell, Oxford, 1967).

   'Notes on Talks with Wittgenstein' *Philosophy Today* No. 1, ed. Jerry H. Gill (Macmillan, New York, 1968), pp. 14–19.

Weil, Simone, *Gravity and Grace* (Routledge and Kegan Paul, London, 1963).

Williams, Bernard, 'Has "God" a Meaning?' *Question*, 1 Feb. 1968, pp. 49–54.

Wilson, Bryan (ed.), *Rationality* (Blackwell, Oxford, 1970).

Winch, Peter, *The Idea of a Social Science* (Routledge and Kegan Paul, London, 1970 edn).

Ethics and Action (Routledge and Kegan Paul, London, 1972).

Wittgenstein, Ludwig, *Tractatus Logico—Philosophicus* (trans. D. F. Pears and B. F. McGuinness) (Routledge and Kegan Paul, London, 1972 edn).

Notebooks 1914–1916 (Blackwell, Oxford, 1961).

The Blue and Brown Books (Blackwell, Oxford, 1969 2nd edn).

Philosophical Investigations (Blackwell, Oxford, 1967).

Remarks on the Foundations of Mathematics (Blackwell, Oxford, 1967).

Zettel (Blackwell, Oxford, 1967).

On Certainty (Blackwell, Oxford, 1969).

Lectures and Conversations on Aesthetics, Psychology and Religious Belief (ed. C. Barrett). (Blackwell, Oxford, 1966).

Philosophische Bemerkungen (Blackwell, Oxford, 1964).

Philosophical Grammar (Blackwell, Oxford, 1974).

Letters to C. K. Ogden (ed. G. H. von Wright) (Blackwell, Oxford, 1973).

Letters to Russell, Keynes and Moore (Blackwell, Oxford, 1974).

'Remarks on Frazer's "Golden Bough"', *The Human World*, May 1971 No. 3, pp. 18–41.

'A Lecture on Ethics' *Philosophy Today No. 1*, ed. Jerry H. Gill (Macmillan, New York, 1968), pp. 4–14.

Zabeeh, Farhang, 'On Language Games and Forms of Life', *Essays on Wittgenstein*, ed. E. D. Klemke (University of Illinois 1971), pp. 328–73.

Zemach, Eddy, 'Wittgenstein's Philosophy of the Mystical' *Essays on Wittgenstein's Tractatus*, ed. I. M. Copi and G. W. Beard (Routledge and Kegan Paul, London, 1966), pp. 359–375.

Ziman, John, *Public Knowledge* (C.U.P., Cambridge, 1968).

Books and Articles not mentioned in the text

Bambrough, Renford, *Reason, Truth and God* (Methuen, London, 1973 edn).

Bartley, William Warren, *The Retreat to Commitment* (Chatto & Windus, London, 1964).

Bell, Richard H., 'Theology as Grammar: Is God an Object of Understanding?' *Religious Studies*, Vol. II, No. 3, Sept. 1975, pp. 307–17

Bildhauer, W. H., *The Reality of God: An Investigation of the Adequacy of Wittgensteinian Fideism* unpublished Ph.D. dissertation, University of Arizona, 1972.

Bouwsma, O. K., *Philosophical Essays* (University of Nebraska 1965).

'Notes on "The Monstrous Illusion" ', *Perkins Journal*, Spring 1971, pp. 5–13.

Coburn, R. C., 'Animadversions on a Wittgensteinian Apologetic' *Perkins Journal*, Spring 1971, pp. 25–36.

Dilley, F. B., *Metaphysics and Religious Language* (Columbia University, New York, 1964).

Edwards, Paul, 'A Critical Examination of "Subjective Christianity" ' *Question* 4, pp. 93–110.

Holland, R. F., 'Is Goodness a Mystery?' *The Human World*, Nov. 1972 No. 9, pp. 1–13.

Holmer, Paul L., 'Indirect Communication: Something About the Sermon (With References to Kierkegaard and Wittgenstein)', *Perkins Journal*, Spring 1971, pp. 14–24.

Hudson, W. Donald, *Wittgenstein and Religious Belief* (Macmillan, London, 1975).

Kenny, A., *Wittgenstein* (Penguin Books, Harmondsworth, 1975).

Malcolm, Norman, 'Anselm's Ontological Arguments', *Religion and Understanding*, ed. D. Z. Phillips (Blackwell, Oxford, 1967), pp. 43–61.

'Is it a Religious Belief that "God Exists"?', *Faith and the Philosophers*, ed. John Hick (Macmillan, London, 1966), pp. 103–10.

Pears, David, *Wittgenstein* (Fontana, London, 1971).

Sutherland, Stewart R., 'On the Idea of a Form of Life', *Religious Studies*, Vol. II No. 3, Sept, 1975, pp. 293–306.

Trethowan, Illtyd, *Mysticism and Theology* (Geoffrey Chapman, London, 1975).

Ward, Keith, *The Concept of God* (Blackwell, Oxford, 1974).

BIBLIOGRAPHY

Books and Articles of biographical interest on Wittgenstein— in addition to those mentioned in the text

Britton, Karl, 'Portrait of a Philosopher', *The Listener*, 16th June 1955, pp. 1071–2.

Drury, M. O'C., 'Ludwig Wittgenstein: A Symposium', *The Listener*, 28th Jan. 1960, pp. 163–5.

Eccles, W., 'Some Letters of Ludwig Wittgenstein', *Hermathena* (Dublin), 1963 No. 97, pp. 57–65.

Fann, K. T. (ed.), *Wittgenstein: The Man and His Philosophy* (Delta Books, New York, 1967).

Gasking, D. A. T. and A. C. J., 'Ludwig Wittgenstein', *The Australasian Journal of Philosophy*, Aug, 1951 Vol. XXIX No. 2, pp. 73–80.

Gass, W. H., 'Wittgenstein—A Man and a Half', *The New Republic*, 22nd June 1968, pp. 29–30.

Heller, Erich, 'Ludwig Wittgenstein: A Symposium', *The Listener*, 28th Jan. 1960, p. 163.

Leavis, F. R., 'Memories of Wittgenstein', *The Human World*, Feb. 1973 No. 10, pp. 66–79.

Leitner, Bernhard, *The Architecture of Ludwig Wittgenstein* (Studio International, London, 1973).

Malcolm, Norman, 'Ludwig Wittgenstein: A Symposium', *The Listener*, Feb. 4th 1960, pp. 207–8.

Mays, Wolfe, 'Recollections of Wittgenstein', *Wittgenstein: The Man and His Philosophy*, ed. K. T. Fann (Delta Books, New York, 1967).

Pascall, Fania, 'Wittgenstein: A Personal Memoir', *Encounter*, Aug. 1973 Vol. XLI No. 2, pp. 23–39.

Rhees, Rush, 'Ludwig Wittgenstein: A Symposium', *The Listener*, 4th Feb. 1960, pp. 208–9.

Review of *Wittgenstein* (W. W. Bartley), *The Human World*, Feb 1974 No. 14, pp. 66–78.

Russell, Bertrand, 'Philosophers and Idiots', *The Listener*, 10th Feb. 1955, pp. 247–8.

'Obituary of Ludwig Wittgenstein', *Mind*, July 1951 Vol. LX No. 239, pp. 297–8.

Index